Making
LEATHER
Purses & Totes

Making
LEATHER
Purses & Totes

Lisa Galvin

Sterling Publishing Co., Inc.
New York

Prolific Impressions Production Staff:

Editor in Chief: Mickey Baskett
Copy Editor: Phyllis Mueller
Graphics: Dianne Miller, Karen Turpin
Styling: Lenos Key
Photography: Jerry Mucklow
Administration: Jim Baskett

Library of Congress Cataloging-in-Publication Data
Galvin, Lisa.
    Making leather purses & totes / Lisa Galvin.
        p. cm.
    Includes index.
    ISBN 1-4027-1475-0
    1. Handbags. 2. Tote bags. 3. Leatherwork. I. Title: Making leather purses and totes. II. Title.

TT667.G35 2005
646.4'8--dc22

2004028502

10 9 8 7 6 5 4 3 2 1

Published in paperback in 2006 by Sterling Publishing Co., Inc.
387 Park Avenue South, New York, N.Y. 10016
© 2005 by Prolific Impressions, Inc.
Produced by Prolific Impressions, Inc.
160 South Candler St., Decatur, GA 30030
Distributed in Canada by Sterling Publishing
c/o Canadian Manda Group, 165 Dufferin Street
Toronto, Ontario, Canada M6K 3H6
Distributed in the United Kingdom by GMC Distribution Services,
Castle Place, 166 High Street, Lewes, East Sussex, England BN7 1XU
Distributed in Australia by Capricorn Link (Australia) Pty. Ltd.
P.O. Box 704, Windsor, NSW 2756 Australia
Printed in China
All rights reserved

Sterling ISBN-13: 978-1-4027-1475-7 Hardcover
        ISBN-10: 1-4027-1475-0

        ISBN-13: 978-1-4027-4060-2 Paperback
        ISBN-10: 1-4027-4060-3

For information about custom editions, special sales, premium and corporate purchases, please contact Sterling Special Sales Department at 800-805-5489 or specialsales@sterlingpub.com.

Acknowledgements

A very special thank you to the following companies for supplying products used to create the projects in this book:

For leather and suede hides, as well as tooling leather, leathercrafting supplies, and tools: Tandy Leather Company®/ The Leather Factory®, Fort Worth, TX 76119, 1-800-890-1611 or 1-877-LEATHER www.tandyleather.com

For rotary cutter, cutting blades (decorative and otherwise), and clear acrylic ruler: FISKARS, 7811 W. Stewart Ave., Wausau, WI 54401, www.fiskars.com

For handles, purse frames, and canvas purses and totes: BagWorks, Inc., 3301-C South Cravens Road, Fort Worth, TX 76119, www.bagworks.com

Baglady Press, Inc., P. O. Box 2409, Evergreen, CO 80437-2409, Toll Free (US and Canada): 888-222-4523, Telephone: 303-670-2177, www.baglady.com

For fabric and gem adhesives: Beacon Adhesives Co., www.beaconcreates.com

For fabric and faux leather trims: Wrights, West Warren, MA 01092, 877-597-4448, www.wrights.com

For rubber stamps: Hampton Art, LLC, www.hamptonart.com

For beading wire and crimp beads: Beadalon®, www.beadalon.com

For acrylic paint: Plaid Enterprises Inc., www.plaidonline.com

About the Artist

Since she pieced her first quilt in her early teens, Lisa Galvin has had a passion for fiber arts and textiles. An artist and designer, she works in a variety of media, from leather to metals to polymer clay and more. Her work can be seen in a variety of craft and art-related magazines and in books as both a solo author and contributor.

Because Lisa loves to teach and inspire creativity in others she conducts workshops and demonstrates for manufacturers and retailers all across the United States. An avid garden and nature lover, she resides in Indiana with her husband and three children.

PERSONAL THANKS

My deepest thanks, love, and regard to my husband, Gary, for his patient support and encouragement during the writing of this book and others. Someone once said to him that it must be hard to live with a creative person. He simply smiled and helped me assemble the large project we were working on together. We've built a lot of things from scratch over the years. I believe that he and our three children are the inspiration and cause for much of my creativity. God has truly blessed me to have all of you in my life! I look forward to the challenges and creative adventures ahead.

Thanks to Kari Lee and The Leather Factory for giving me the opportunity to bring my love of fiber arts into the realm of leather. Thanks for sharing your knowledge, experience, and friendship with me over the years!

Many thanks to Mickey Baskett, my editor, for her patience and for giving me the opportunity to share my love of leather with others through the writing of this book!

Thanks to Lee, Rosie, and Ray at the Indianapolis Tandy Leather Store for all of your helpful tips and advice. Your love of people and of leather is evident; we're fortunate to have you and Tandy in Indy!

To my creative colleagues - Debba, Katie, Vicki, and Mary - I offer my heartfelt thanks for keeping me inspired to try new things and push my limits!

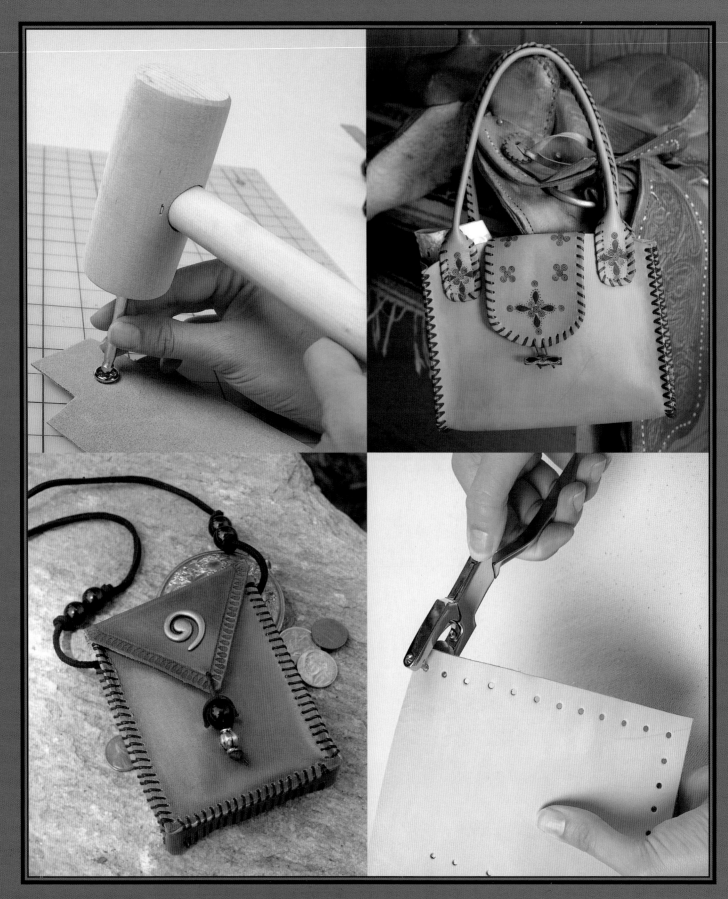

Table of Contents

Introduction
8

Supplies & Techniques
10

A Little About Leather, Types of Leather, Working Surfaces,
Tools, Surface Embellishing Tools, Hardware

Construction Techniques
24

Working with Patterns, Cutting Leather, Machine Stitching, Handstitching

Purse & Tote Projects

Metric Conversion Chart
126

Index
127

Manmade materials and fabrics just can't compare with leather - a durable, supple fabric from nature. Who can help but stroke soft garment or upholstery grade leathers, or brush a hand over the velvet-like surface of cow or pig suede, or enjoy the pleasant, unmistakable scent of leather goods?

I'm a fiber artist by trade, and I might never have made the connection between creating with cloth and creating with leather had it not been for a leather company representative who saw my work at a trade show and asked if I might be interested in working with the company's products. Three weeks later, when a sample box of leather goods arrived at my doorstep, I questioned my initial enthusiasm. It took another three weeks of touching, feeling, flexing, and turning a piece of suede before I actually worked up enough courage to actually make something with it. Working with leather has been a labor of love ever since!

That was five years ago. Like any new material or medium, leathercrafting is a learn-as-you-go process. Through trials, errors, and learning from teachers, books, and magazine articles, I've completed more than 100 leather projects, and fear of cutting and working with this fascinating material is a thing of the past. This is my hope for you as well!

This book includes projects designed to teach you about the many attributes, tools, and techniques used in leathercrafting. You'll quickly discover numerous ways to create and embellish purses, totes, and other clothing and household items with leather skins and hides. From tooling to branding, punching, cutting, and stitching, both beginners and more advanced leather-crafters can find inspiration through the projects, tips, and useful ideas presented.

As your knowledge and skills grow, so also will your collection of tools designed specifically for leathercrafting. And you will assemble an assortment of leather and suede pieces - remnants of previous projects. In this book, you'll find beautiful projects that can be created using these pieces that are too precious to discard. Some that you won't want to miss are the Purse of Many Colors, the Gypsy Quilted Purse, and the Cigar Box Purse.

Beginners will enjoy trying the Quick Catch Handbag or attempt tooling for the first time on the Dragonfly Garden Seed Pouch. Once comfortable with tooling, you may be inspired to create a companion piece, the Dragonfly Garden Tool Tote!

Be sure to see what's concealed inside our Alligator-Grained Handbag! You're in for a surprise - and you can use the technique to explore other possibilities, shapes, and sizes.

Whether you seek to become a master leather-crafter or just to enjoy making a few projects, you will find a wealth of information and many like-minded and knowledgeable leatherworking friends through one of these groups:

The International Internet Leathercrafters Guild
http://iilg.org/

International Federation of Leather Guilds
http://www.ifolg.org/members.htm

Contact your local leather store to find out if a guild meets in your area.

Enjoy creating the purses and totes presented here for your personal enjoyment and as gifts for the special women in your life!

Lisa Galvin

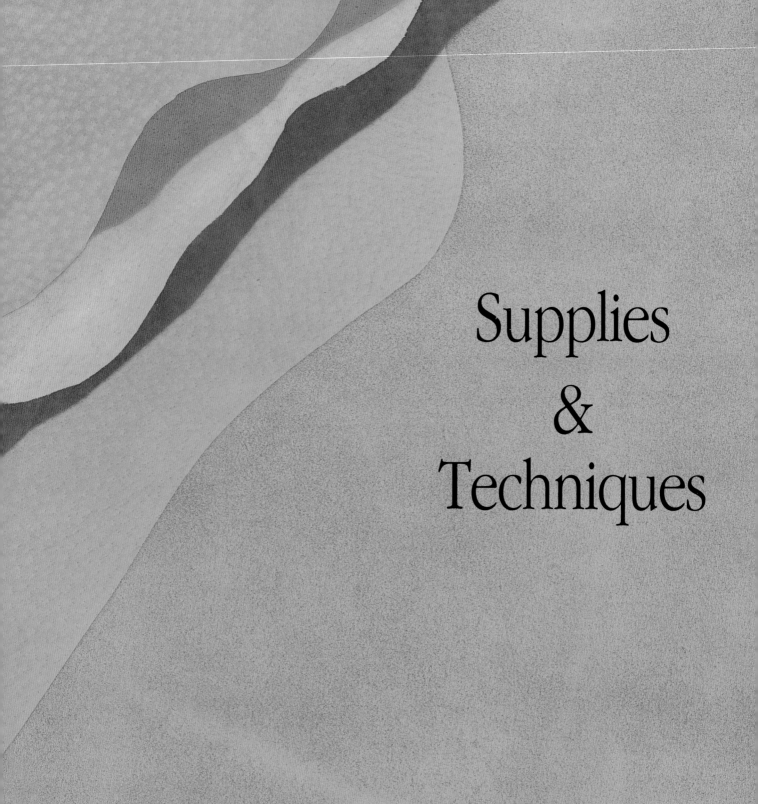

Supplies
&
Techniques

This section includes information about buying, using, storing, and crafting with different types of leather. You'll also see and read about tools and supplies you need for cutting, sewing, and decorating leather.

A Little About Leather

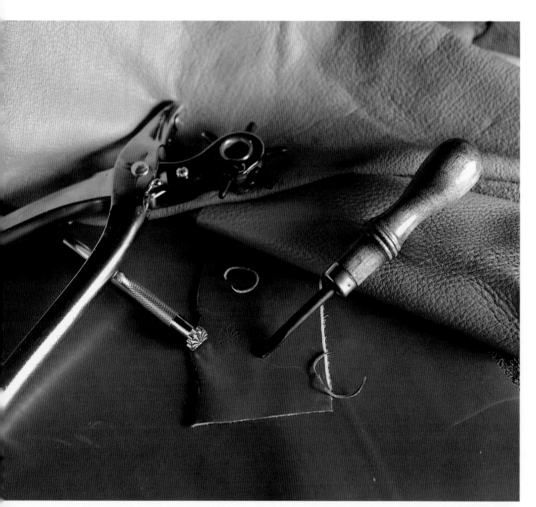

Leathers available on the market today are a by-product of the meat industry. First, the hair, epidermis, and underlying flesh layer are removed. What is left is the middle layer, called corium. Corium is tanned using smoke or chemical or natural vegetable baths to produce the soft, supple, durable leather we enjoy.

The flesh side, called a split, is used to create suede or embossed leathers such as the alligator-grained cowhide used in one project in this book. Embossed leathers often can be purchased at a fraction of the cost of exotic skins, and endangered species are preserved.

"Skin" is the common term for a pelt smaller than a cow; larger, cow-sized pelts are referred to as hides. Skins are usually sold whole. Hides also can be purchased whole (for upholstery or garment use) or, as is the case with vegetable-tanned and nature-tanned cowhide, hides can be purchased in smaller sections referred to as the belly, side, shoulder, and so on. Each smaller section of the hide offers different characteristics and qualities; they should be selected based on your project needs.

Sold in a variety of sizes and thicknesses, leather is typically sold by the square foot. Prices vary, depending on the overall surface quality, the type of leather, and the thickness, which is measured in ounces. Thinner leathers, at one to two ounces, are lightweight, affordably priced, and suitable for projects receiving light to moderate use. The heaviest leathers, at ten to eleven ounces, are tooling leathers that are used for carpenters' belts and harnesses, where rugged durability is essential.

Leather and suede in cord-like strips called **"lacing"** are also available by the roll or in packages of smaller lengths. Lacing can be used for attaching leather pieces together or for trimming techniques.

WHERE & HOW TO BUY LEATHER

Smaller leather pieces are available in fabric and department stores, but for a selection of size, type, quality, and colors consult on-line sellers and catalogs or look in the leather or shoe repair section of your phone book.

To determine the hide or skin size needed for any project, first determine the dimensions (in inches) of the piece(s) you need. Convert this measurement to square feet this way:

1. Multiply the length (in inches) by the width (in inches). The result is the total square inches of the piece.
2. Divide the total square inches by 144. The result is the total square feet.

Even if a pattern was not designed for leather (like many commercial purse, pillow, and home furnishings patterns), you can use this formula to determine how much leather you need.

BUYING TIPS

- Because leather is natural, regardless of where you purchase it, you will find blemishes, holes, and some flawed areas. You may prefer to avoid them entirely or to use only in or on specific areas of your project. For best results, purchase a hide with slightly more square footage you need so you'll have more flexibility when placing pattern pieces and cutting.
- Just as with fabric and wallpaper, dye lots can vary, as does leather itself. For larger projects where two or more skins or hides are needed, purchase all the pieces together to ensure colors and grain will match from piece to piece.
- Remnant bags offer an inexpensive way to get started with working in leather. Available in a wide range of leather types, scraps are a good way to experiment with new techniques without purchasing full skins or hides.
- Leather should not be stored in airtight plastic bags as this can result in damage and encourage mold. Leather should be allowed to breathe.
- Store leather flat, if possible. Roll skins and larger hides to prevent creasing caused by folding.

TYPES OF LEATHER

Vegetable-Tanned Cowhide

Size, quality, and overall affordability make vegetable-tanned cowhide (veg-tan) a good, general purpose choice yielding a good-sized, flat surface that can be used for many types of projects. Most novice leather workers prefer to begin with a section of the hide referred to as a premium tooling shoulder, and that's what I recommend.

Like blank canvases, ready and waiting to be transformed, vegetable-tanned leathers are among the most versatile of all leather types. "Veg-tan" can be carved, tooled, branded, or cut to create intricate designs and patterns, or left as is. Initially tan-colored, this form of leather is very absorbent so it quickly accepts dyes and stains as well as acrylic or textile paints. When working with vegetable-tanned leather, be sure to keep your hands and work surfaces clean and oil-free.

Nature-Tanned

This light golden-brown-toned leather can be used much the same as its vegetable-tanned counterpart. Already a warm and pleasing color, stains and dyes can bring out the grain and add dimension around edges.

Upholstery or Garment Grade Leathers

Ranging in thickness from one to five ounces, thinner weights of this type of leather are easily stitched on a conventional sewing machine. They are available in assorted natural-toned colors.

Suede

With a velvety soft textured surface, both cow and pig suedes are available in assorted colors, including vibrant aqua, purple, and red. Pig suede is the lighter weight of the two; this soft, somewhat fuzzy leather is relatively inexpensive and a great place to begin working with leather.

Kidskin

Terrific for small projects, the supple feel of these small skins make it a personal favorite. Kidskin is easily stitched using a home sewing machine; many projects can be created quickly and easily from each skin.

WORKING SURFACES

Cutting Mat

Designed specifically for use with a rotary cutter, a self-healing cutting mat is a "must-have" for anyone serious about working with leather. They come in a variety of sizes with printed measurement grids. Use a clear acrylic straight edge (with measurement grid printed on) to make straight, exact cuts every time.

Stone Slab

A 1-1/2" (or thicker) piece of marble or granite is the perfect surface for stamping, punching, and tooling leather, creating a solid work surface with little bounce. To prevent a stone slab from breaking, place a poly punch board on top.

Poly Punching Board or Wooden Cutting Board

Similar to kitchen cutting boards, these soft surfaces are essential when using drive punches or stitching awls - they allow the tips of the tools to penetrate the leather layer(s) for a clean cut. The boards also may be used for stamping and tooling. For best results, place a poly punch board on a stone slab before punching. This greatly reduces the amount of bounce, giving you cleaner cuts and speeding the punching and stamping process. TIP: If a stone slab is not available, try placing the punch board on a flat concrete surface for punching and tooling.

Cutting mat

Stone slab

TOOLS

Although you don't need to buy everything at once, as you work with leather you'll likely want some specialized tools that will save you time and expand your leathercrafting capabilities. Some basic tools you will find useful are shown here.

Pictured left to right: rotary hand punch, swivel knife, rotary cutter, ruler, scissors.

Tools, continued.

Leather Shears

With their razor sharp edges, leather shears cut easily through even thick leathers, providing a nice, clean cut. They're best for use on short or curved cut edges; longer, straight edges are best cut with a rotary cutter and straight edge. Reserve your leather shears for use on leather only so you preserve the cutting edge for years of use.

Rotary Cutter

Available with straight and a variety of decorative cutting blades, rotary cutters create a clean, straight edge every time. Use them with a cutting mat and straight edge ruler.

Craft Knife

This tool can be used to cut thin leather. It must be sharp.

Using a rotary cutter on a cutting mat.

Using an edge beveller to shave off an edge.

Edge Beveller

You can remove sharp cut edges from vegetable- or natural-tanned leathers using a shaving tool called an edger or edge beveller. Available with a flat or concave back side, this tool has a grooved tip with cutting edge between the grooves. Slide it along edges, top and bottom, of leathers weighing at least 4 oz.

Slicker

A slicker is rolled or slid across the lightly dampened, cut edges of 4 oz. to 11 oz. leathers to leave a slick, finished look.

Drive Punches

These sharp edged cutting tools are struck with a mallet to drive through leather, creating holes and perforations of various sizes and shapes. The most commonly used ones are round hole drive punches.

Round hole drive punches can be purchased individually, in sizes from 1/16" to 1" in diameter. Most beginners find that the mini set (5/64" to 11/64") and maxi set (3/16" to 5/16") with their interchangeable cutting tips serve them well.

Pronged chisel and diamond punches are specialized tools that are used for a more finished appearance when using ultra thin leather lacing or when saddle stitching pieces together.

Filigree-shaped punches offer endless possibilities - they can be punched through all types of leather, from very lightweight velvet pig suede to heavy

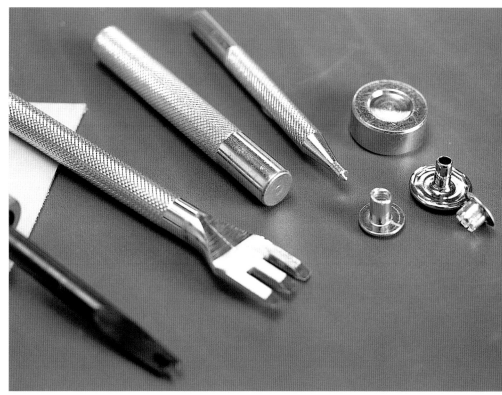

An assortment of drive punches.

hides. Heart, crescent, diamond, square, and other shapes can be used singly or with round hole punches to create decorative effects. (For an example, see the Cell Phone Pouch.)

TIP: For best results, practice your pattern on poster board, then position the pattern on leather, using a binder clip to hold it in place, and punch, using the poster board as a template.

Mallet

With wood or rawhide versions available, a mallet is preferred for stamping or punching leather. Metal hammers can damage punches.

Hand Punches

These rotary style punches that make round holes are available in sizes ranging from pinhole to 7/32". They are typically used to punch stitching holes. The rotary wheel can be turned to adjust the hole size. This type of punch should be used near edges.

Tools, continued.

■ Over-stitching Spacer Wheel

If creating your own patterns and leather designs is for you, then you will find this a handy tool - it can mark an even line of spaced stitches that can later be punched with drive punches or a stitching awl. The tool is rolled along a straight edge ruler or near edges to be stitched, leaving a slight imprint as well as a groove for threads to rest in. For best results, dampen leather with a sponge before use.

Wheels in various sizes are available; the most common are sizes 5, 6, and 7.

Overstitching spacer wheel

■ Awls

Awls, which have pointed tips of assorted sizes, are used to make perforations, usually for stitching. There are also specialized awls for handstitching. This type of awl has a needle tip and carries a spool of thread. It can be used much like a sewing machine for stitching thick layers of leather together.

■ Binder Clips & Fabric Weights

Because holes pierced through leather and suede are permanent, patterns or pieces being stitched are clipped together with **binder clips** along the edges to prevent shifting during cutting and stitching. Binder clips are commonly found in office supply stores.

For cutting larger pieces, use **fabric weights or heavy books** to hold patterns in place during cutting.

SURFACE EMBELLISHING TOOLS

Leather is porous, and the leather surface easily picks up color in the form of dyes, stains, or paints as well as oils from your hands. For this reason, your hands and your work area should be clean when working with leather.

■ Woodburning Tool

A woodburning tool can be used to mark, accent, or "brand" leather, penetrating the soft surface to leave a darkened imprint. A wide selection of tips is available.

- Remove hot tips using needlenose pliers. Place the tips on a metal baking sheet to prevent burning your work surface when switching tips.
- Periodically sand off the charred buildup that collects on tip ends as you work, using fine grit sandpaper.

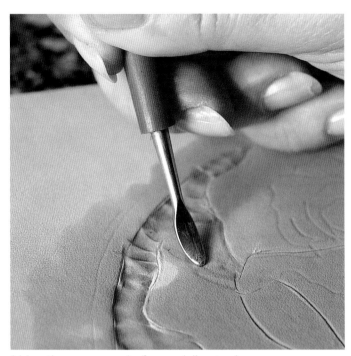

Using the spoon end of a modeling tool.

Stylus & Modeling Spoon

Available in several styles and sizes, these tools can be used alone or with stamps to create a variety of effects. Use them to trace patterns on cased leather, create hairlines, bevel the edges of a design, or make impressions. Once stained or dyed, impressed areas pick up pigment, providing contrast.

Swivel Knife

Use a swivel knife to cut grooved lines into leather, carving the surface. Hold your finger on the rounded top edge to maneuver along pattern lines or for freehand designing.

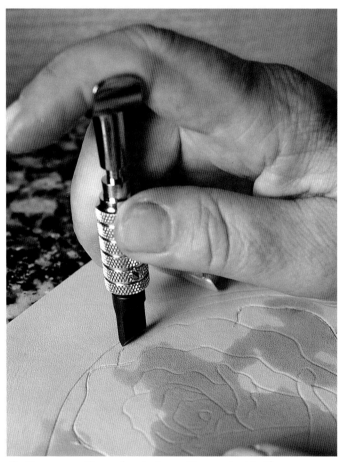

Cutting an outline of a design with a swivel knife.

Woodburning tool

Surface Embellishing Tools, continued.

■ Leathercrafting Stamps

A basic tool set contains the commonly used stamps: seeder, beveller, background, camouflage, pear shader, and scalloped veiner. These tools allow you to explore techniques used in both simple and complex tooling designs.

It's amazing what can be done with a few simple stamping tools and techniques, from alphabet stamps, which can be used to personalize anything from purses to wallets and luggage tags, to filigree patterns, weaving, animal shapes, and more.

TIPS FOR SUCCESSFUL STAMPING

• Case leather by dampening surface with a sponge. This will soften the surface, allowing it to be more flexible and make a better imprint. CAUTION: Using too much water (saturating the leather completely) will cause the stamp to cut the surface of the leather when you stamp.

• For best results, hold the tools perpendicular to the work surface and strike the opposite end of the stamp with a mallet.

• When using a background stamp to create shaded areas, move the stamp slightly as you work, "walking" it along the surface so that the background pattern is consistent and the outer shape of the stamp is not visible when you are finished.

ABOVE: Stamping Tools & Supplies, *pictured from left to right:* Modeling tool with spoon modeler at one end and stylus at the other; an assortment of tooling stamps. At the top, a poly mallet and a piece of granite, which can be used as a stamping surface.

RIGHT: Tooling scallops outside the border of a design.

Rubber Stamps

Because of their popularity for cardmaking and scrapbooking, there is a plethora of rubber stamps available. Rubber stamping is amazingly easy and can transform plain or colored leathers of all types into patterned works of art in no time!

Using Ink: Best results are achieved with permanent, pigment, or solvent-based inkpads recommended for fabric and leather. Test the ink first on the leather you're using to be sure the color works well and gives a sharp image and to determine drying time needed. Some pigment inks require extended drying and/or heat setting. New chalk-based permanent inkpads are also available.

Using Acrylic Paint: Pour a small amount of acrylic paint on a foam plate and mix with fabric medium as directed by paint manufacturer. Dip cosmetic sponge in the paint, daub off excess, and load stamp. Stamp on leather. Repeat, applying paint to stamp before stamping again unless otherwise directed.

Stamping leather with permanent ink.

Dyes & Stains

Dyes and stains, the most common methods of coloring leather, are available in water- and spirit-based versions. Generally, stains tend to streak, and dyes provide more even coverage. NOTE: Marred, scratched, and tooled areas of a design pick up color differently; take this into consideration when selecting leather for a project.

TIPS FOR DYEING & STAINING

- For smaller leather pieces use a swab, a soft cloth, or a piece of sheep's wool. Apply the color using a swirling motion. On larger surfaces, apply using a paint brush.

- Always apply dyes and stains to a larger piece of leather than needed as leather shrinks as it dries. Once cut to actual size, apply color carefully to the cut edges, using a paint brush or soft cloth. Don't saturate the cloth - this can cause the leather to absorb too much color at edges, marring the previously stained surface.

- Several light applications of stain or dye are preferred over one heavy coat. Allow the leather to dry between applications.

- Use a scrap piece of paper or plastic to protect your work surface.

STAMPING TIPS

- Work on a smooth surface.

- Press stamp on inkpad, then stamp on leather, pressing down firmly with your palms so all portions of the image make good contact with the surface. Remove and repeat as needed.

- Do not rock stamp from side to side - this can distort the image.

- Try combining punches, stamping, and tooling with rubber stamping for unusual dimensional effects!

- Acrylic paint and a fine-tip paint brush or fabric markers can be used to color inside stamped images.

BELOW: Acrylic craft paints, leather dye, artist's paint brushes.

Surface Embellishing Tools, continued.

Paints

Acrylic paints and fabric paints offer easy ways to add colorful accents to leather. **Always** test the paint on a scrap of your project leather and allow to dry. The leather should remain flexible after painting, and the paint shouldn't crack. For best results, add textile medium to acrylic paint when using on leather or purchase paints specifically designed for use on leather and fabrics. Drying times can vary.

For design painting: Apply paints using paint brushes.
For stamping: Use a cosmetic sponge to dab paint on the stamp.
For stenciling: Apply paint with a stencil brush or cosmetic sponge.

Antiquing Finish

Antiquing is a wonderful way to accent tooled or stamped designs. Simply brush an antiquing finish made for leather or acrylic paint on the prepared leather surface and quickly wipe off the excess before it dries. The paint color or antiquing will be left in the tooled, stamped, or cut areas and in the leather's lightly patterned natural grain. TIP: For best results, practice on a scrap piece of leather that has been stained or dyed to match your project.

Leather Finishes

A variety of methods can be used to seal and finish leather, protecting it for long use. For best results, follow manufacturer's instructions and use only sealers recommended for use on leather to ensure flexibility. Suedes should not be sealed.

Apply sealers and waxes with a soft cloth, then polish or spray for a durable finish.

Adhesives

Contact cement or **leathercrafting cement** are the two best glues to use on leather. They create a permanent bond and provide maximum adhesion, but allow leather to maintain its flexibility. **Fabric glue** also can be used; however, test the glue - some tend to become hard and brittle over time.

Spread glue in a thin layer, using a brush or a small piece of card stock. This helps prevent excess adhesive from oozing into the design. If a specific width of cement or glue is to be applied, use repositionable sticky notes to define the area to prevent excess glue from being brushed beyond where it is needed.

Fringes & Trims

With so many styles to choose from, the hardest part is deciding which one to use! These added embellishments can be stitched on (for best long-term results) or glued on with an appropriate glue. Instructions for attaching embellishments are included in the individual project instructions.

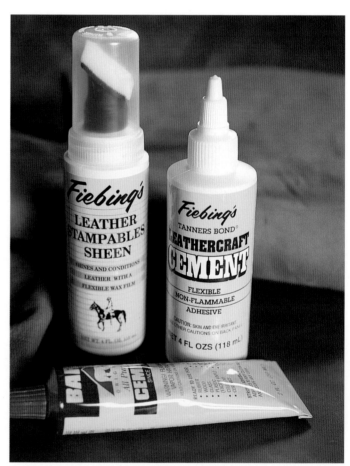

Leather finish and two types of adhesive.

HARDWARE

Take full advantage of the wide assortment of possibilities that hardware offers to your work with leather. Check the scrapbooking and paper crafting sections for ideas - eyelets and snaps, grommets galore, decorative buttons and brads are just a few of the items.

Eyelets

For best results use eyelets with a backing liner similar to those found on grommets. Use a round hole drive punch in a size slightly smaller than the eyelet's center hole. Slip the eyelet through the front side of the leather, slip on the backing liner, and set the back using an **eyelet setter**.

Grommets

Typically larger than eyelets, grommets are installed in a similar fashion. For best results, use a **grommet setter** with a base to fit the grommet size.

Snaps

Snaps are attached with snap setting tools designed specifically for the size of the stamp. Most snaps come in kits, with the **setting tool** and snaps in the same package.

Spots

Available in a wide assortment of styles, colors, and finishes, spots have sharp, pointed prongs on the back and may contain rhinestones. To insert, position as desired, pressing lightly to mark prong location on the leather. Cut small slits with a craft knife or chisel drive punch, insert the prongs through the slits, and fold to overlap at center.

Clasps & Purse Latches

You'll find a wide variety of styles of clasps and latches for closing purses. The pronged edges of magnetic clasps and purse latches are marked on leather the same way as spots. A thin metal plate is slipped over the prongs before folding them.

Clasps and latches with rounded inside edges should be positioned and marked for placement. Cut with a craft knife, drive punch, or both before attaching to handbag and flaps.

Attaching snaps

Construction Techniques

In this section, you'll learn how to work with patterns and cut leather. You'll also learn about stitching leather by machine and by hand, including descriptions of the most common hand stitches and how to make them.

WORKING WITH PATTERNS

Patterns and punching guidelines (called punch templates) should be photocopied
and can be enlarged if needed as called for in instructions.

Making Pattern Templates

You will need to make a template for all patterns you will be using.

You will need:

Scissors
Pencil or ink pen
Spray adhesive or tape
Copier
Poster board

Here's How:

1. Copy patterns from book onto copy paper using a copier.
2. Attach copies to poster board using spray adhesive or tape.
3. Cut out around pattern to make template.
4. To use template, place onto leather and trace around template using a sharpened pencil or ink pen for darker colors.

Steps to Create Easy Enlargements

Use this method to enlarge patterns if the finished size will be larger than 8-1/2" x 11" or 8-1/2" x 14".

1. Photocopy the pattern.
2. Use a black marker to make several reference points at various areas of the photocopied pattern. I typically mark A, B, C, D, and so on, working around many areas of the pattern and at the center in no particular order.
3. Place the photocopied pattern back on copy machine and set to the enlargement needed (200%, 300%, etc.). Make a copy. (Only a portion of the original pattern will show on the enlargement.)
4. Reposition the original photocopy on the copy machine and enlarge another area. Repeat until all areas of the original pattern have been enlarged.
5. Piece the copied enlargements together like a jigsaw puzzle, matching the marked reference points. TIP: Use a light box (or a glass window or door on a sunny day) to help in aligning reference points.
6. Tape the pieces together, keeping all reference points aligned, and cut out along outer pattern lines, taping as needed to hold the pieces together.
7. Attach to poster board with spray adhesive or tape. Cut out the enlarged pattern or punch template.

Positioning

Leather has a face as well as back side. Usually it is easy to distinguish them, except on some suede pieces. If you're not sure which side is the face, I recommend using the side you prefer.

For best results, position all pattern pieces on the leather before making any cuts. As much as is possible, position portions of the pattern that will be most visible on the finished project on the most attractive areas of the skin or hide, avoiding marks or unsightly areas. To prevent stretch, position patterns in the direction of the backbone, from head to tail.

Cutting Leather

Choosing the best means of cutting leather depends largely on the project. Smaller pattern pieces can easily be cut out using a sharp craft knife or leather shears, allowing you to manipulate as you cut. Larger pieces are best cut on a cutting mat using a straight edge clear acrylic ruler and rotary cutter.

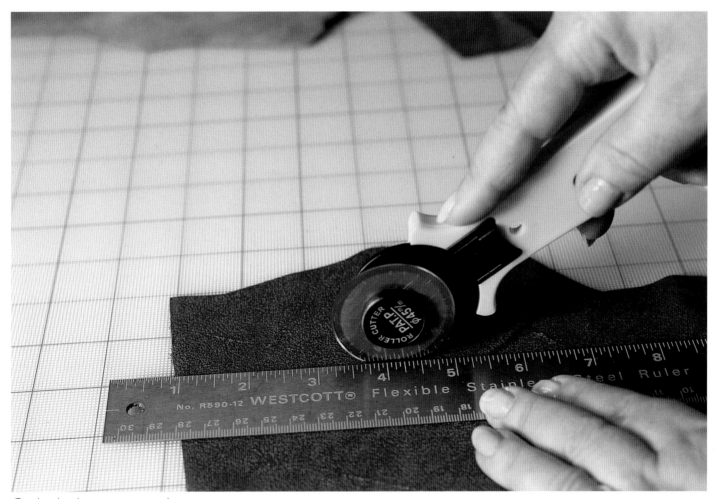

Cutting leather on a mat using a rotary cutter.

Rounded or curved edges of thicker weight leathers can be cut with a craft knife - make several stroke-like cuts along same line before penetrating completely.

Tight curves can first be punched with a round hole drive punch that fits the curved pattern edge. Cut the remaining straight or slightly curved edges using a rotary cutter or craft knife. See the Dragonfly Garden Tool Tote for an example.

MACHINE STITCHING

Thinner-weight leathers can be sewn on a standard home sewing machine. Refer to the machine manual for recommended settings, and adjust the presser foot and tension for the type and thickness of leather being stitched. For best results, test using scrap leather, layered like your project (two, three, or more layers). Set the stitch length to 8 to 10 stitches per inch. (Stitching holes closer together than this make a perforated seam that can tear.)

Needle sizes for sewing leather typically range from size 14 for lightweight suedes to size 18 for some moderately heavyweight leathers. For best results, always begin your project with a new needle, as dull tips can cause tearing. Consult the manual with your sewing machine to find proper size of needle needed.

Do not use straight pins to hold pieces of leather or suede - once the leather is perforated, the holes are there to stay! Instead, use binder clips to clamp pieces together. To prevent marring the leather surface, insert a small piece of scrap leather between the clip edge and your project surface. Remove the binder clips as you stitch.

Never backstitch at beginning and end when machine stitching leather. To secure, leave 4-5" of thread at the beginning and end of the stitched seam. Bring the thread ends over the outside edge or pull to the back side and tie in one or more square knots. Apply a dot of glue to the knot to further secure it.

A variety of seam finishes can be used to create clean, professional-looking seams on leather, including French seams, flat-fell, mock flat-fell seams, among others.

HANDSTITCHING

Although hand stitching can be used on all leather weights; medium to heavy weight leathers are often too thick to stitch on a conventional home sewing machine. Aside from the aesthetic appeal that any type of handwork gives, many times hand stitching is simply the best and only method of assembling some projects. As with anything else, having the right tools to work with on any given project is essential. Preventing frustration, the correct needle can often be a huge time saver, and in the end lead to a better quality finished project. Following are types of needles that can be used for hand stitching:

• **Glovers needle:** This needle comes in a variety of sizes, however, most commonly used are sizes #1 and #3. With a sharp 3 sided point; it easily pierces leather for easy stitching.

• **Sharps:** Great for beading; these needles come in a variety of sizes.

• **Large eye needle:** Also referred to as an embroidery or upholstery style needle, these typically having a somewhat blunt tip as well as a large eye that can accommodate heavy threads, fibers or yarns. They're great for stitching through pre-punched holes in leather.

• **Two-prong lacing needle:** This specialized needle is designed for use with flat leather or vinyl lacing from 3/32" to 5/32" wide. Pronged portion of the needle is opened slightly, allowing lace end to be inserted; prongs are then released to trap the lace between the needles' two layers. For best results, trim lace end before inserting into pronged portion of needle; tapering the side edges on this end only to an arrow-like point. Close prongs and lightly tap the pronged portion of the needle with a mallet on a solid surface to press prongs into the lace; gripping it tightly and preventing it from slipping out during stitching.

A variety of handstitching and lacing techniques can be used to add decorative edges to single layers of leather or to join two or more pieces. Handstitching is done through holes that are punched in the leather. You can use an awl and a punching board to make the holes or use a rotary hand sewing punch. If you enjoy handstitching, quilting, or beading on lightweight leathers, the rotary hand sewing punch is a time and finger saver. It will create consistent needle-size holes up to 5/64" quickly and easily.

Common Hand Stitches

Double-back Stitch -
With this method needle is brought through first stitching hole in area directed or at one side edge; leaving a 1 - 3" tail on back side. Whipstitch once; going through first two holes before stitching in and out of pre-punched holes, trapping the tail be-

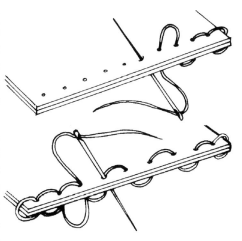

tween the layers. At the end, return to the original starting point, going through opposite side of same holes so that when finished, the seam appears to have been stitched on a home sewing machine. Once back at starting point, whipstitch once, then thread needle in and out of stitches between the two layers. Trim ends.

Running Stitch -
Stitched similar to double-back stitch, but at the opposite end, you do not return to the starting point. Secure thread ends same as with double-back stitch.

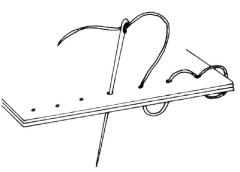

Whipstitch -
A threaded needle is slipped through at least two hole perforations or into stitching in an area that will not be seen from the top side to secure ends. This technique also can be used to

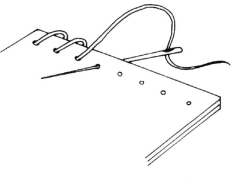

stitch along outer edges of leather by bringing needle from front side of leather, around edge and through the back side of next hole or perforation. Pull excess to front then continue along edge. For added interest, at the end turn and stitch back to the original starting point, leaving a criss-crossed line of stitching at edge.

Saddle stitch - Appearing much like the double back stitch, this method uses two needles to stitch a machine-type stitch. Cut a length of thread three times the seam length (length needed may vary depending upon lace thread and thickness). Thread ends through separate needles and, beginning on one end, stitch, bringing needles through each hole or perforation until you reach the opposite end. Tie thread ends to secure. It is helpful to use a stitching pony to hold the leather while you work.

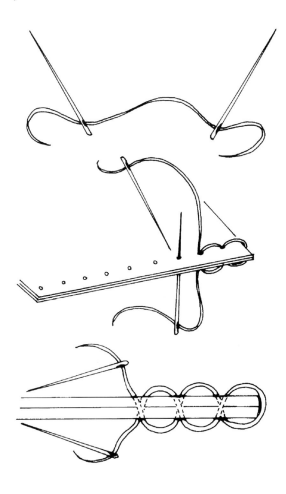

Light to medium weight velvet pig suede and garment leathers can be stitched fairly easily using a glover's needle. Whipstitch to secure ends, going through previous holes or stitches to secure. Thread laced needle in and out of stitching 1-2", then trim threads.

Purse & Tote Projects

In this section, you'll see how to make 20 purse and tote projects. Some are made completely of leather, others are leather-trimmed. All showcase the natural beauty of leather and a variety of leathercrafting techniques. Each project includes a complete list of supplies and tools that you need and step-by-step instructions, plus photographs, patterns, and diagrams.

BEACH TOTE

Fresh and funky flowers with rolled suede lace accents liven up an otherwise plain purchased straw handbag. Enlarge or reduce the pattern to fit your purse.

SUPPLIES

Leather:

4" x 4" cow suede scraps, assorted colors

1/8" suede lacing, hunter green and tie-dyed bright colors

Other Supplies:

Straw purse

Permanent fabric glue

Spray adhesive

Poster board

Tools:

Scissors

Pattern

Sharpened pencil or ink pen

INSTRUCTIONS

Prepare & Cut:

1. Photocopy flower pattern, reducing or enlarging as needed. Make pattern templates. Transfer pattern to cow suede, using a sharpened pencil to trace around edges. TIP: For darker colors, an ink pen may be necessary. (Photo 1)

2. Remove pattern and cut just inside the traced lines so that no lines are visible on the finished flowers.

Contiued on page 34

Photo 1 - Tracing around the pattern.

Assemble:

1. Glue suede flowers to purse front, using the photo as a guide.

2. From tie-dyed lacing, cut three lengths 3-1/2" to 4-1/2". Tightly roll from one end to the other to create flower centers. Apply a small dot of fabric glue to the end to secure and hold briefly, until the glue sets.

3. Glue these coils of lacing to centers of flowers.

4. To make S-shaped accents, cut three 6" to 7" lengths of hunter green lacing. Working from one end, roll the lace toward the center, then roll in the opposite direction from the other end to make the S-shape. Secure each end with a dot of glue and hold until set.

5. Glue accents to front of purse, using the photo as a guide. ❏

Patterns for Beach Tote & Key Ring
(actual size)

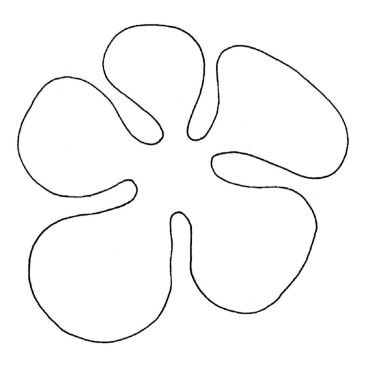

FLOWER KEY RING

Pictured on Page 33

SUPPLIES

In addition to the supplies and tools listed for the Beach Tote, you will need:

Leathercrafting cement

Art glitter

Key ring

1/4" dowel, 8" long

Baking sheet

Home oven

Toothpick

Scrap paper

INSTRUCTIONS

1. Using the flower pattern used for the tote, cut out a suede flower.

2. From tie-dyed lacing, cut a length 3-1/2" to 4-1/2". Tightly roll from one end to the other to create the flower center. Apply a small dot of glue to the end to secure and hold briefly, until the glue sets.

3. Glue to center of flower.

4. Punch a 5/32" hole near outer edge of one petal.

5. Use a toothpick to apply a thin bead of cement to highlight areas of flower. Sprinkle with art glitter, shake off excess on a scrap piece of paper, and return to container. Lay flat until dry.

6. Attach key ring through 5/32" hole.

7. Preheat oven to 225 degrees Fahrenheit. Cut a 20" length of Hunter Green suede lacing. Dampen with water, then wrap around dowel, overlapping at ends to hold tight to dowel when released. (Photo 2)

8. Place on a baking sheet and bake for 10 minutes. Remove from oven and let cool. Remove the lacing from dowel and tie the center point of the lacing strip around the metal key ring. Tie a knot to secure. ❑

Photo 2 - The dowel wrapped with green lacing.

CANVAS HANDBAG
WITH LEATHER TRIM

It's amazing what effect a bit of embellishment can have. This handbag, which has a decided western flair, takes only one hour to create.

SUPPLIES

Leather:

28" two-strand braided black leather trim

15" black round lacing, 2mm

Other Supplies:

Black curve-top canvas shoulder bag

2 horsehair tassels, 2"

2 aged synthetic bone beads, 3/4"

Silver finish concho, 1-1/2"

Contact cement

Tools:

Ruler

Binder clips

Dressmaker's chalk wheel or pencil

Round hole drive punches, 11/64" (5mm) and 5/64" (2mm)

Wooden mallet

Poly cutting and punching board

Brayer *or* metal roller, 1-1/2" wide

Leather shears

Flat-blade screwdriver

Plain shoulder bag, braided trim, tassels, beads.

continued on page 38.

continued from page 36

INSTRUCTIONS

Punch:

1. Measure, then mark a line 1" from top of handbag on both sides, using a dressmaker's chalk wheel or pencil.

2. Using the 11/64" drive punch and mallet, punch a hole at center-front of bag, 1" from top. (This will be used to attach concho.)

3. Using the 5/64" punch and mallet, punch two holes side by side, 1/2" below the concho hole. (These are for attaching the beaded tassels.) (See Photo 1)

Assemble:

1. Apply cement to back of the braided leather trim. Apply a band of cement slightly narrower than the braided trim on the bag over the penciled line. Let set briefly.

2. Beginning and ending 3/8" from the concho hole at the bag front, adhere braided trim, pressing the cement-coated surfaces together first with fingers, then rolling with a brayer to ensure good contact.

3. Slip round lace through a bone bead, through the loop of one tassel, and back through the bead. Bring lace ends together, adjust to make even, then pull to slide bead over tassel loop. Tie an overhand knot at top of bead. (Photo 2)

4. Slip ends of lace through one of the 5/64" holes, then tie an overhand knot on inside of handbag to secure. Trim ends. Repeat for second tassel, slipping ends through remaining 5/64" hole.

5. Attach concho by screwing it in place through the 11/64" hole. ❑

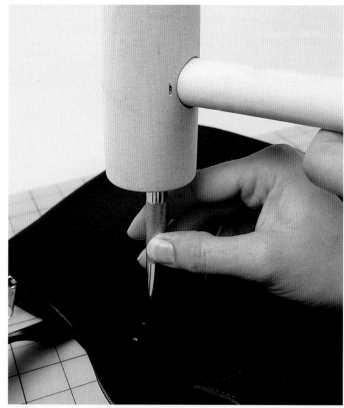

Photo 1 - Punching holes in purse with a punch and mallet.

Photo 2 - Tying an overhand knot after sliding the bead over the tassel loop.

DRAWSTRING HANDBAG OR BACKPACK

Whether hung over your shoulder as a tote or used as a backpack, this durable upholstery grade leather handbag with grommet and drawstring features is simple to create and easily stitched on a home sewing machine.

Instructions begin on page 40.

SUPPLIES

Leather:

Brown upholstery grade leather
    15-1/2" x 24-1/4" rectangle
    8-1/2" square

90" black latigo leather lacing

Other Supplies:

Poster board

Spray adhesive

10 antique brass grommets, 3/8"

10 black acrylic beads, 1/2"

Accent charm or pendant

Large round locking slider, black

Contact cement

Scrap paper

Brown nylon thread

Tools:

Sewing machine with size 18
    needle (or appropriate needle
    for your machine)

Cutting mat

Straight edge ruler

Rotary cutter

Round hole drive punch, 3/8"

3/8" grommet setter

Permanent black marker, fine
    point, *or* dressmaker's chalk
    wheel

Scissors

INSTRUCTIONS

Cut:

1. Photocopy the circle pattern for bottom, attach to poster board with spray adhesive, and cut out.
2. Center pattern on back side of 8-1/4" leather square and trace around edges, using a marker. Remove pattern. Use leather shears to cut along traced line.

Construct:

1. Use a permanent black marker and a straight edge ruler to measure and mark a line 6" from one 24-1/4" edge of leather piece. This will be the top.
2. With right sides facing, binder clip the short (15-1/2") sides of bag piece together. Machine stitch 5/8" from edge, removing the clips as you stitch. Do not backstitch. Knot thread ends to secure.
3. Create a mock flat-fell seam by trimming one seam allowance to 1/8". Press 5/8" seam allowance over the 1/8" seam. Cement to inside of bag; concealing the trimmed seam allowance between the two layers. Roll with a brayer to smooth and ensure good contact.
4. With wrong side of bag facing up, machine stitch 1/4" from first seam, stitching through the bag and 5/8" seam layers to reinforce seam and hold flat. Knot thread ends.

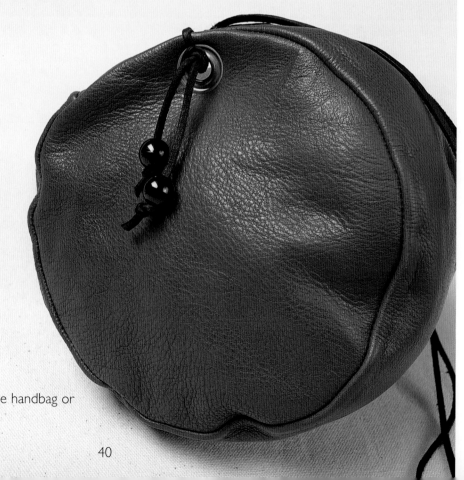

RIGHT: Bottom of the handbag or backpack.

5. Using the line marked in step 1, apply contact cement to the inside top 6". Let dry as directed, then fold top edge to the marked line, pressing the cement-coated sides together as you work your way around the bag. Use a brayer to press flat.

6. With right sides facing, binder clip bottom circle to bottom edge of bag. Machine stitch the pieces together using a 5/8" seam allowance, removing binder clips as you stitch.

7. Trim seam allowance on bag side to 1/8" so when the bag is turned right side out the seam allowance from bottom of bag will cover the trimmed seam.

8. Apply contact cement to seam allowances. Apply a 1/2" band of cement to the corresponding inside edges of bag. Allow to dry briefly, then turn right side out, pressing cement-coated seam allowances to inside edges of bag as you work your fingers around the bottom. Roll with a brayer to press flat.

Punch & Install Grommets:

1. Create reference points for punching grommets, beginning 2" on either side of seam and 1-3/4" from top edge of bag. Measure and, with the marker, make nine small dots 2-1/2" apart.

2. Place bag on punch board with top edge open. One at a time, center the 3/8" round hole drive punch over dots and punch, using a mallet, through the cemented leather layers. Repeat as needed, working your way around the top edge of the bag.

3. Use the grommet setter and mallet to insert grommets.

4. For bottom strap attachment, pinch side and bottom edges of bag together, place on punch board, and use the mallet to punch a 3/8" round hole approximately 1/2" from the pinched edge.

5. Use the grommet setter and mallet to attach grommet.

Install Lacing:

1. Beginning on outside of bag at a grommet nearest the side

Pattern for Bottom
(Enlarge @165% for actual size.)

seam, weave latigo lace in and out of the grommets, slipping beads and decorative pendant accent on the lace on the outside of the bag. Bring lace end back through the first grommet, bring ends together, pull to make even, and insert through locking slider. Pull lacing, pinching slider to draw top of handbag together.

2. Adjust lacing length as desired for backpack and tie an overhand knot.

3. Insert one lace end through grommet at bottom of bag. Bring lace ends together and tie another knot, pulling so both knots are close to grommet.

4. Slide a bead on each lace end and knot to hold in place. Trim excess lace. See photo. ❏

QUICK CATCH HANDBAG

This handbag resembles a skirt with its fun fringed bottom, button accents, and laced edges.
It's a great get-acquainted-with-leather project for beginners.

SUPPLIES

Leather:

2 black cow suede pieces,
8-1/2" x 11"

10" black suede lacing, 1/8"

3/32" grained vinyl lacing

Other Supplies:

Wood beaded handle

2 round wooden buttons, 1"
diameter

Oblong wooden button with
shank, 1-1/4" long

2 solid brass Chicago screws, 1/4"

Brown sewing awl thread

Spray adhesive

Poster board

Tools:

Rotary cutter

Cutting mat

Straight edge ruler

Binder clips

Craft knife

Seam gauge

Leather shears

Round hole drive punches, 3/32",
5/32", and 1/4"

Poly cutting and punching board

Glover's needle

Two-pronged lacing needle

Supplies pictured: suede pieces, beaded handle, buttons, vinyl lacing.

continued on page 44

continued from page 42

INSTRUCTIONS

Cut:

1. Photocopy patterns with punch and cut guides and enlarge pattern as directed.
2. Attach patterns to poster board with spray adhesive. Cut out, using a craft knife and straight edge ruler.
3. Using a rotary cutter, cutting mat, and straight-edge ruler, cut both cow suede pieces to 8-1/2" x 10".
4. Using binder clips, clip handbag pattern to one suede piece. Place on punch board. Use the mallet and 1/4" drive punch to punch hole at top center. Punch remaining holes shown using a 3/32" drive punch.
5. Cut fringed bottom with craft knife. (Photo 1) Remove pattern.
6. Repeat steps 4 and 5 on second 8-1/2" x 10" piece.
7. Use a binder clip to clip the handle straps pattern to one of the remaining 1" x 8-1/2" suede pieces. Use shears to cut two strap ends.
8. Punch strap as shown on pattern, using the 1/4" drive punch.
9. Cut four 1/2" squares of suede. Punch a 1/4" hole at the center of each. (These will be used as "washers," adding the thickness needed to secure the Chicago screws.)

Stitch Vertical Seams:

1. Overlap 10" side edges of two handbag pieces, lining up punched holes and using binder clips to hold in place.
2. Cut a 35" length of vinyl lacing and thread on the two-pronged needle. Beginning at first hole at top of handbag, bring needle up from between the overlapped layers, stitching through top layer only, leaving a 3" tail that will be caught between the two layers, concealing it as you stitch. Whipstitch a couple of times over top edge, going through the first hole in both layers to secure. Pull taut. Take the needle through the second hole, stitching through both layers.
3. Continue to sew the overlapped pieces together, using a running stitch and weaving the tail end in and out of the stitching as you go.
4. When you reach the bottom, bring the needle through back side of corresponding holes on opposite overlapped edges, pull taut to bring bottom of handbag together, and stitch to top of other side. Whipstitch twice, bringing the needle through only one punched hole the second time. Weave the threaded needle in and out of stitching between layers to secure. Cut excess lace.

Photo 1 - Cutting the fringe.

Stitch Bottom & Top:

1. Binder clip bottom edge at sides to keep punched holes aligned correctly. Thread the two-pronged needle with 15" of vinyl lacing. Beginning on one side, bring needle up from between layers, stitching through one hole only and leaving a 3" tail. Whipstitch once, then sew bottom edge closed using a running stitch. Secure both ends as before. Cut off excess.
2. Cut a 60" length of vinyl lace and thread on the two-pronged needle. Beginning on the inside near one side edge, bring needle through one punched hole, leaving a 3" tail. Whipstitch once in same hole, then continue to whipstitch entire top edge; catching the 3" tail within the stitches on inside of handbag as you go to secure. Back at the starting point whipstitch again, going through the last hole. Weave needle through stitching on inside of purse for about 3". Cut off excess lace.

Attach Buttons:

1. Thread glover's needle with awl thread. Handstitch round buttons in place through punched holes. Whipstitch two to three times on inside of purse to secure stitching. Cut excess. Repeat for remaining button.

2. Attach oblong button used for closure by stitching through lacing holes at center front, 5/8" from top edge.

3. Place back of handbag on punch board. Measure 5/8" from top edge, then punch one 5/32" hole on each side of overlap.

4. Tie a knot in one end of 10" black suede lace piece. Beginning on inside of handbag, insert remaining suede lace end through one of the 5/32" holes and bring back to inside through second hole. Adjust length so it slips easily over the oblong button. Tie a knot, then cut excess.

Attach Handle:

1. Beginning on outside of handbag, insert Chicago screw post through one hole in punched handle strap. Slip on a 1/2" suede "washer," then insert through hole at one side edge. Slip on another 1/2" suede "washer." Loop strap through handle's wooden ring. Secure strap to purse, slipping the screw post through remaining hole on strap end. Insert screw back and tighten with screw driver.

2. Repeat on other side. ❑

Patterns for Quick Catch Handbag

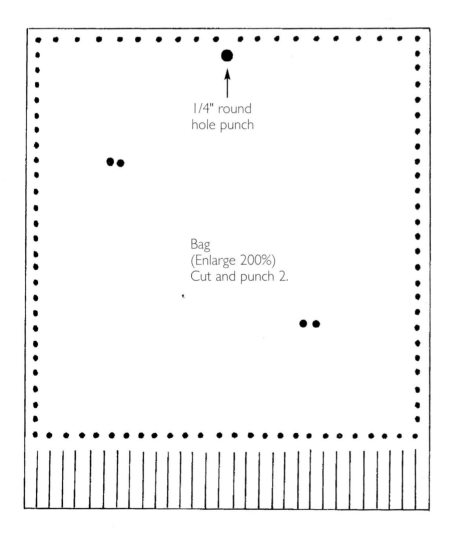

1/4" round
hole punch

Bag
(Enlarge 200%)
Cut and punch 2.

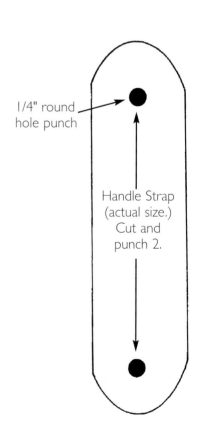

1/4" round
hole punch

Handle Strap
(actual size.)
Cut and
punch 2.

Leather:

Beige cow suede, 8-1/2" x 9-1/2" for flap and outside pocket

2-3 oz. vegetable tanned leather, 6" x 8-1/2" for inside pocket

60" brown round leather lacing, 2mm

Other Supplies:

Denim tote bag, 13-1/2" x 11-1/2" x 5-1/4"

Border stencil

Acrylic craft paint - Brown oxide

Textile medium

50-75 brown 1/8" eyelets

4 snaps, #24

2 aged synthetic bone beads, 3/4" long

Poster board

Spray adhesive

Optional: Black foamcore poster board, cut to fit bottom

Fine point black permanent marker

Tools:

Rotary cutter with straight blade

Cutting mat

Straight edge ruler

Leather shears

Binder clips

Straight pins or pattern weights

Round hole drive punches, 5/32" (snaps), 3/32" (eyelets), 1/8" (lacing)

Mallet

Poly cutting and punching board

Snap setter & anvil

Eyelet setter

Stencil brush

Foam plate

Water basin

Paper towel

Craft knife

DENIM TOTE WITH POCKETS

This tote's suede closure and pockets, placed inside and outside, are easily removed so the tote can be machine washed. There are three snaps on the flap closure so that it can be unsnapped for easy removal. Lacing would be undone to remove outside and inside pockets for washing.

Supplies pictured: tanned leather, border stencil, acrylic craft paint, stencil brush.

Instructions begin on page 48.

INSTRUCTIONS

Cut:

1. Photocopy pocket pattern with punch guide (see page 51). Attach to poster board with spray adhesive. Cut out.

2. Using the cutting layout as a guide, position pocket pattern near one end of cow suede piece. Binder clip pattern to suede. Cut using rotary cutter, cutting mat, and straight edge ruler. This is the outside pocket.

3. From remaining suede, cut a 3-1/2" x 7-3/4" piece for the closure flap. Use a craft knife and straight edge ruler to cut and remove a 3/4" x 1-1/4" rectangle from two corners.

4. If needed trim the tanned leather piece to 6" x 8-1/2" for inside pocket.

Punch:

1. Using the cutting layout diagram as a guide, punch three 5/32" holes in the closure flap. These are for snaps.

2. Position flap at top of tote and mark placement of holes, both front and back, on the tote using a fine point marker. Remove flap. Punch the corresponding 5/32" snap holes in denim at the marks.

3. Binder clip pattern-punch guide to the 6" x 8-1/2" cow suede outside pocket piece. Place on punch board and punch stitching holes, using a 1/8" drive punch and mallet.

4. Punch round hole for pocket snap, using 5/32" drive punch. Remove pattern.

5. Binder clip pattern-punch guide to the 6" x 8-1/2" vegetable tanned inside pocket piece. Place on punch board and punch stitching holes, using a 1/8" drive punch and mallet or a rotary punch tool. (Photo 1)

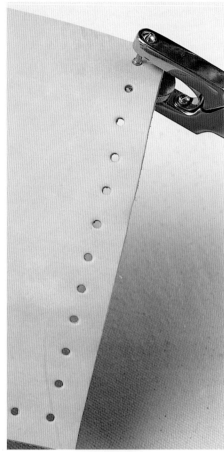

Photo 1 - Punching the stitching holes of inside pocket.

Cutting Layout

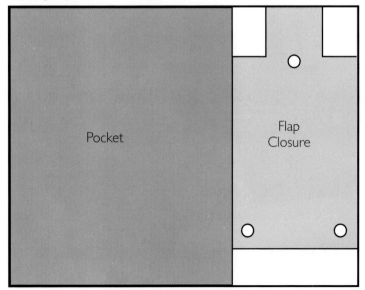

Pocket

Flap
Closure

Photo 2 - Stenciling the flap.

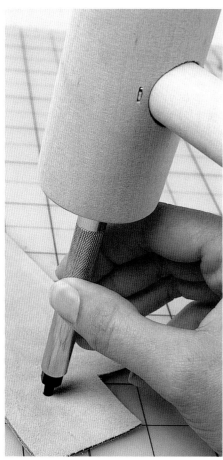

Photo 3 - Making a hole for a snap on the flap.

6. Insert punch board inside tote. Position pocket pattern-punch guide on tote. Use straight pins or pattern weights to hold punch guide in place during punching. Punch snap hole and stitching holes in tote to match cow suede pocket piece.

Stencil:

For best results, clean stencil with a paper towel or damp cloth before stenciling another area of suede.

1. On a foam plate, mix equal amounts of brown oxide paint and textile medium. These snaps are used on the flap so that it can be easily removed for washing. The outside pocket snaps onto the tote. There is no snap on the inside pocket.

2. Position stencil at one side edge of suede flap. Load stencil brush with the paint mixture and gently dab off excess. Using a pouncing motion, stencil the decorative accent on both sides of flap. (Photo 2) Set aside to dry.

3. Position stencil near top of suede pocket between side stitching holes. Using the same paint mixture, stencil the design. Let dry.

Install Snaps & Eyelets:

1. Position and set all snaps on cow suede pieces and denim tote. (Photos 3 through 6) Three snaps are used on the flap so that it can be easily removed for washing. The outside pocket snaps onto the tote. There is no snap on the inside pocket.

2. To reinforce the denim and prevent fraying, use an eyelet setter to set an 1/8" eyelet in each stitching hole on the tote.

continued on next page

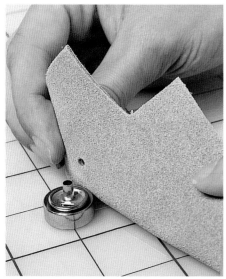

Photo 4 - Placing the bottom part of a snap.

Photo 5 - Placing the top part of a snap.

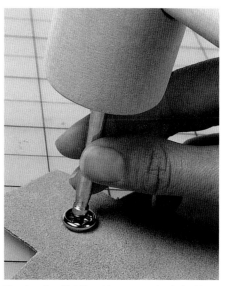

Photo 6 - Setting the snap to join the two parts.

continued from page 49

Construct:

1. Cut a 30" length of round brown lacing and tie a knot in one end. Snap outside pocket to tote bag to hold in place while you stitch the inner and outer pockets to the tote at the same time, sandwiching the denim between the pockets. Insert the straight end of the lace through the hole in one top corner of the inside pocket, then through the corresponding eyelet in the tote, then through suede pocket on front. Continue lacing as shown in Figs. 1 and 2. Pull taut at center near snap. Tie an overhand knot, slip synthetic bone beads on lacing, and knot ends.

2. Snap flap in place at top of tote bag.

3. Use a craft knife and straight edge ruler to cut black foamcore board to fit bottom of bag. Insert in bag bottom. (Photo 7) ❑

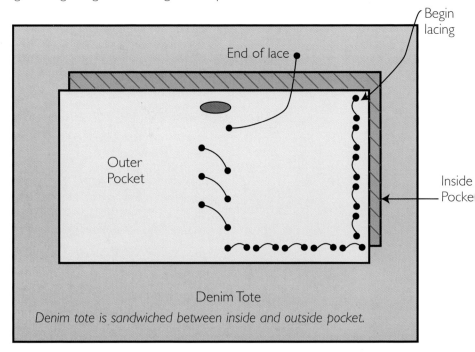

Fig. 1 - Beginning the stitching on the pockets.

Begin lacing

End of lace

Outer Pocket

Inside Pocket

Denim Tote

Denim tote is sandwiched between inside and outside pocket.

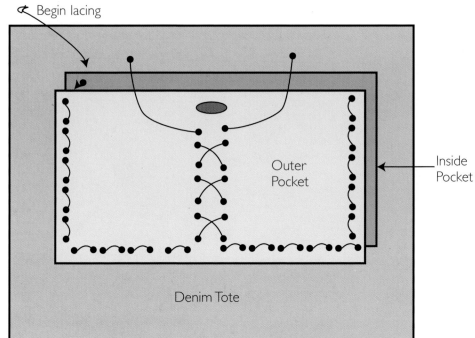

Fig. 2 - Completing the stitching on the pockets.

Begin lacing

Outer Pocket

Inside Pocket

Denim Tote

Photo 7 – Inserting foamcore in bottom of bag.

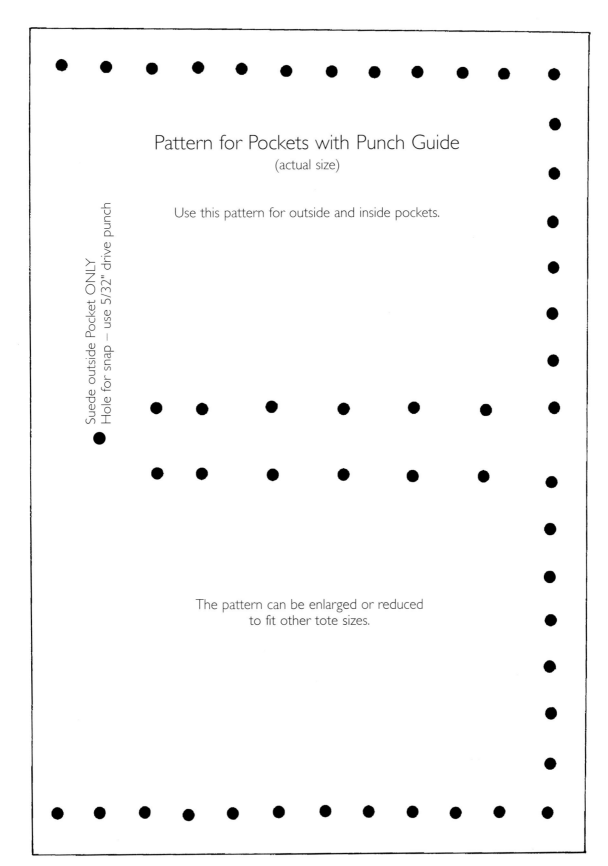

Pattern for Pockets with Punch Guide
(actual size)

Use this pattern for outside and inside pockets.

Suede outside Pocket ONLY
Hole for snap – use 5/32" drive punch

The pattern can be enlarged or reduced
to fit other tote sizes.

SUPPLIES

Leather:
8 pieces vegetable tanned, 2-3 oz. leather, 2-1/2" x 2-1/2"
24" length black round lacing, 2mm
Black doe kidskin leather

Other Supplies:
Unfinished wooden cigar style box, 10-3/4" x 2-3/8" x 7-1/8"
Acrylic craft paint - Rose pink, bright magenta
Decoupage medium, matte finish
Rubber stamps - Background text, postcard, postmarks
Multi-surface chalk inkpads - Red brick, cloud white
Acid-free archival solvent inkpad - Black
Pink faceted acrylic stones, assorted sizes and shapes
24" silver jewelry wire, 20 gauge
1" black button
Black ribbon, 5/8"
Black felt
Contact cement
Leather adhesive

Tools:
Scratch awl *or* spacer set with #5 over-stitching wheel
3-in-1 bone folder/creaser/slicker
1/8" drive punch
Mallet
Poly punch board
Leather shears
Scissors
Card stock
Pencil
Water basin
Clear acrylic ruler
Drill
Drill bits, 5/64", 1/8"
Fine grit sand paper
Tack cloth
Steel wool
1" wash style paintbrush
Foam plate
Paper towel
Scrap paper
Coloring brush tool *or* cotton swab *or* cosmetic sponge Brayer
Round nose jewelry pliers
Wire cutters

CIGAR BOX PURSE

Vegetable tanned leather and rivet-adorned imitation leather bias tape are attached to a cigar box purse that's given a beaded handle. Rubber stamped accents and faceted jewel embellishments give the overall design a nostalgic appeal.

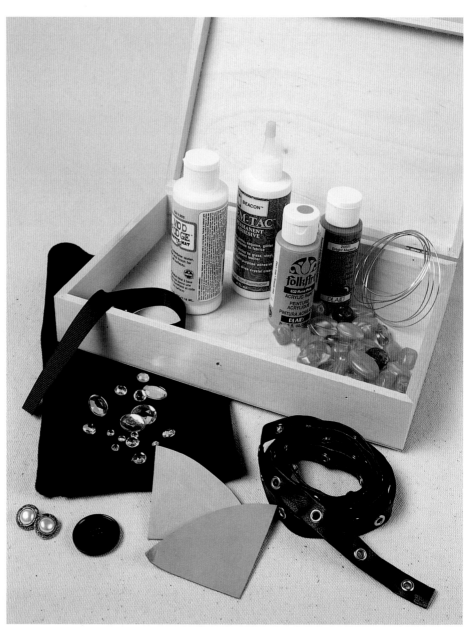

Instructions begin on page 54.

52

INSTRUCTIONS

Cut & Prepare:

1. Photocopy or trace pattern for leather corner pieces, enlarging or reducing as needed to fit your box.
2. Cut out and trace on cardstock. Cut on traced lines.
3. Use a pencil to trace the pattern on the back side of the eight vegetable-tanned leather pieces. Cut out, using leather shears.
4. Dampen leather with water and place on a flat surface. Use a ruler and the pointed tip of a scratch awl to impress faux stitch holes in the leather, approximately 1/4" from all outside edges. (The holes need not completely perforate the leather.) *Option:* Use a spacer set with a #5 over-stitching wheel. Let leather dry completely.
5. One piece at a time, lightly dampen edges only of each leather piece. Run slicker back and forth along edges until smooth. Set aside to dry. Repeat on remaining pieces.
6. Using a 1/8" drill bit, drill one hole on side of box opening for beaded knob closure.
7. Using the 5/64" drill bit, drill holes for beaded handle wires approximately 1-3/4" from each side.
8. Lightly sand entire surface of cigar box, inside and out, using fine grit sand paper to remove any roughness. Wipe with a tack cloth to remove all traces of dust.

Paint:

1. Pour a good amount of rose pink paint on a foam plate or palette. Use a 1" paintbrush to apply a generous coat of paint to inside and outside of box. Let dry.
2. Lightly sand with steel wool to smooth grain raised by the paint. Wipe with a tack cloth. Apply a second coat of rose pink. Let dry. Lightly sand again with steel wool, if needed, and wipe with a tack cloth.
3. Mix a small amount of magenta with the rose pink. Paint the top and side edges of all leather corner pieces with this slightly darker color. Place on a scrap piece of paper to dry.

Stamp:

1. Use the black inkpad to stamp the front and back of box randomly with stamps of your choice. Also stamp some of the leather corner pieces. TIP: For an interesting effect, use a torn piece of paper to mask a part of the box and stamp the image so it's on both the paper and the wood. Remove the stamp and paper to reveal a stamped image with a jagged edge. Let dry. (Photo 1)
2. Use white and brick red chalk ink to add highlights to the stamped box, using a coloring brush tool, cotton swab, or

Photo 1 - Stamping the box, using a piece of paper as a mask.

cosmetic sponge. (Photo 2) Let dry.

Decorate Outside:

1. Use a 1" paintbrush to apply one to two generous coats of decoupage medium to the outside of the box. TIP: Create the look of canvas by brushing the decoupage medium in different directions.
2. Use adhesive to glue leather pieces at corners, front and back. Let dry.
3. Apply another coat of decoupage medium over both leather and wood surfaces. Let dry completely.
4. Cement eyelet-adorned bias tape to edges of box as shown in photo. Begin and end at the bottom of the purse, over-lapping ends slightly. TIP: Aligning an eyelet hole with the hole drilled for the closure will allow the lace to be pulled through easily.

Make Handle:

1. Insert one end of silver wire in one of the 5/64" holes on the top of the purse. Use round nose jewelry pliers to twist end on the inside of the box to secure.

2. Slip beads on wire in random order, covering most of the wire to create the handle.
3. Slip opposite end of wire through remaining 5/64" hole and twist wire on inside of box. Pull taut to secure handle in place. Cut excess wire with wire cutters.

Make Closure:
1. Cut a 6" length of 2mm round lace and knot one end.
2. Slip remaining end through 1/8" hole drilled on widest top edge of box. Slip on a small button, followed by a 1" button, then a large acrylic bead. Knot end to hold in place.
3. Cut an 8" length of round lace and tie a knot in one end. Beginning on inside, bring through 1/8" drilled hole on opposite side. Slip on a large acrylic bead, then knot end to hold in place.
4. To close purse, wrap long lace end around button-and-bead-adorned lace several times, wrapping as shown in photo.

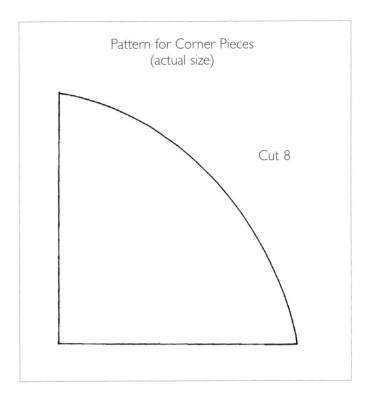

Pattern for Corner Pieces
(actual size)

Cut 8

Photo 2 - Using chalk ink to add highlights to the stamped box.

Cut Lining:
1. To determine lining size, open box and measure, then cut, a one-piece paper pattern to fit lining area. (Fig. 1) Add 1" to total to allow for expansion along hinged edge when purse is open.
2. Use the paper pattern to cut black felt lining. Set pattern and felt aside.

Create Gussets:
The side edges of the gussets will be cemented to the inside of the purse, lining those edges and preventing the purse from opening fully so the contents won't fall out.

1. With purse open, measure height along inner side edge. Subtract 1/2" from this measurement - this is the gusset length. With purse standing upright, hold open and measure how open the purse needs to be for easy

continued on next page

continued from page 55

access. Add to this measurement the size of the edges of the box (that's where the gussets will be cemented). Use these dimensions to cut two rectangular gussets from kidskin leather.

2. Place kidskin on a scrap piece of paper. Apply a 2" band of contact cement to back side of leather along top edge. Cut a piece of grosgrain ribbon slightly longer than the leather's width. Apply contact cement to ribbon, center, and adhere 1" from the top edge, leaving a short length of ribbon (approximately 1/2") extending beyond each side. (Fig. 2)

3. Fold leather over straight side edge of ribbon, pressing cement-coated areas together. Roll with a brayer to smooth.

4. Along that area of gusset bottom that will not be attached to side edges of inner box, use 1/8" drive punch, mallet and punch board to punch a series of holes approximately 3/8" from bottom edge, 1/4" apart.

5. Cut an 8" length of 2mm round lace and tie a knot in one end. Beginning on back side of leather, thread lace through stitching holes, pull tightly to gather the bottom edge. (Fig. 2) Knot remaining end to hold. Set aside.

Finish Inside:

1. Use a brush to apply one to two coats of decoupage medium to those inside edges that will not be lined with felt or leather. Let dry.

2. Attach felt liner inside the purse by brushing a thin coat of decoupage medium onto the wood surface. Work quickly to press the felt in place before medium dries. Smooth with your palms.

3. Cement gathered gussets to inside edges of wood as shown in Fig. 3, applying cement to face side of leather and coating only those portions of the side edges that will be adhered to wood. Press together. Let dry.

Decorate:

1. Glue faceted acrylic stones of various sizes and shapes to box front. Buttons may also be attached. Use wire cutters to cut and remove button shanks. Let dry completely.

2. Repeat on back side. ❑

Fig. 1 - Determine desired opening for purse.

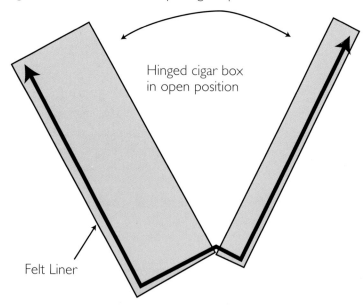

Fig. 2 - Fold top 1" of kidskin over a length of grosgrain ribbon. Punch along bottom and thread lacing through holes to gather.

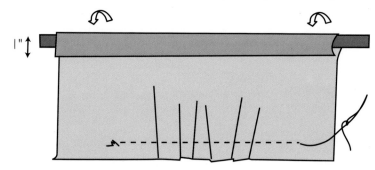

Fig. 3 - Side view of kidskin gusset installed in purse.

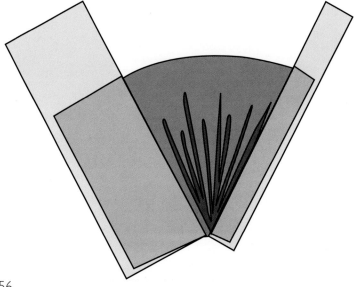

Patterns for Red Velvet Suede Tote

Instructions begin on page 58.

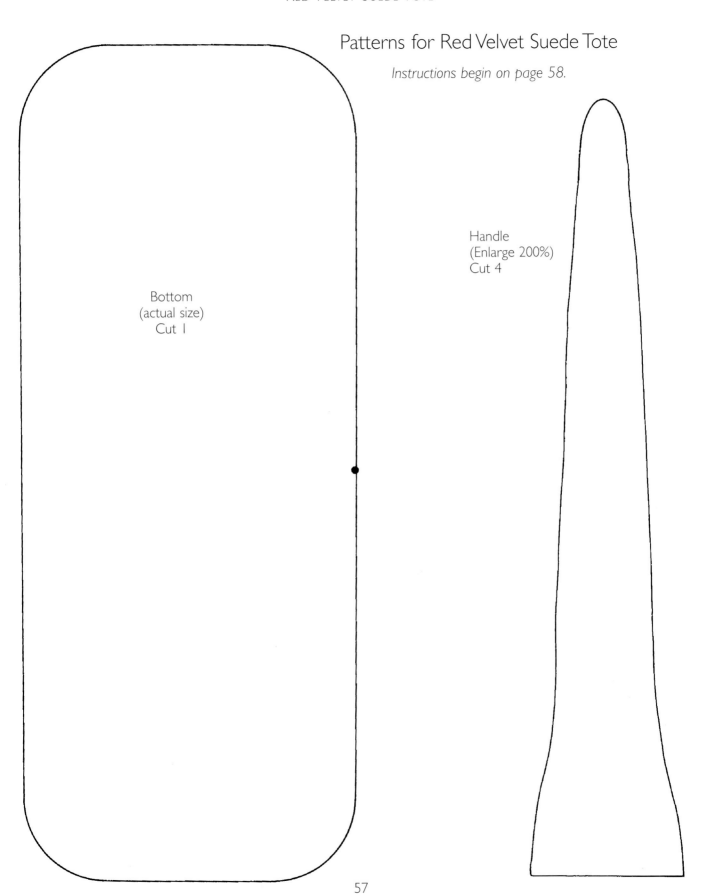

Bottom
(actual size)
Cut 1

Handle
(Enlarge 200%)
Cut 4

SUPPLIES

Leather:

Red velvet pig suede
  1 piece, 12" x 22" (for side edges)
  1 piece, 3-1/2" x 9" (for bottom)
  4 pieces, 16" x 3-1/2" (for handles)
2-3 oz. vegetable tanned leather,
  3-1/2" x 9" (for tote bottom)

Other Supplies:

Rubber stamps - Small face frame,
  square face frame, "Diva,"
  "Oooh-la-la"
Multi-surface chalk inkpads - Red
  brick, cloud white
Acid-free archival solvent inkpad -
  Black
Nickel-finish diamond spots, 3/8"
Permanent jewelry adhesive
Leathercrafting cement
Fuzzy gimp braid, 5/8" wide
28" decorative fiber trim
1/2 yd. black lining fabric
1/2 yd. black iron-on interfacing
Sewing thread - Black, red
Poster board
Spray adhesive
Brass magnetic bag clasp
Fabric adhesive

Tools:

Ink pen
Rotary cutter
Cutting mat
Clear acrylic ruler
Straight pins
Craft knife
Leather shears
Binder clips
Scissors
Sewing machine with size 11 and
  size 18 needles (or applicable
  size needles for your machine)
Sewing needle
1/4" dowel
Iron
Ironing board

RED VELVET
SUEDE TOTE

Rubber stamped faces and words decorate this dramatic suede tote.
Diamond-shaped spots add silvery gleam; fuzzy gimp braid trim on the
stamped images gives the look of a hat or hair. All the stitching is done
on a sewing machine.

Instructions begin on page 60

Supplies pictured: Diamond-shaped spots, fuzzy gimp braid

continued from page 58

INSTRUCTIONS

Cut:

1. Photocopy patterns (on page 57) for handles and purse bottom. Enlarge handle pattern as directed. Attach to poster board using spray adhesive. Cut out.

2. Place red suede pieces face (fuzzy side) down on a flat surface. Position patterns. Trace pattern outlines on back side of leather with ink pen.

3. Cut out pieces, using leather shears:
   From 16" x 3-1/2" piece, cut four handle pieces
   From 3-1/2" x 6" piece, cut one purse bottom piece
   Mark dot for center.

4. Trace bag bottom pattern on back side of vegetable tanned leather piece with an ink pen. Mark a second line 3/8" inside of traced line. Cut out.

5. Use a rotary cutter and cutting mat to cut one 12" x 22" piece each of red suede, lining fabric, and iron-on interfacing.

6. Using the pattern, cut one purse bottom piece from both the lining fabric and interfacing. Use pins to hold pattern during cutting.

Construct Bag:

1. Place the 12" x 22" red suede piece on a flat surface, face (fuzzy side) up. Stamp randomly with black ink, using the photo as a guide and stamps of your choice. Let ink dry.

2. Press pointed wing ends on diamond spots on suede, placing the diamond spots randomly around the stamped images. Remove, revealing a mark on the suede. Use a craft knife to cut small slits at marks. Insert the wing ends of each diamond spot through the slits and, one at a time, use a 1/4" dowel to press the wings flat on the back side of suede, overlapping at the center of the spot. Repeat for all.

3. With right sides together, binder clip 12" side edges of red suede. Use a sewing machine with the size 18 needle threaded with coordinating thread to machine stitch 3/8" from edge, removing binder clips as you stitch. **Do not** back stitch. To secure ends of thread, tie ends into square knots. Add a drop of adhesive to secure knot, and trim excess thread.

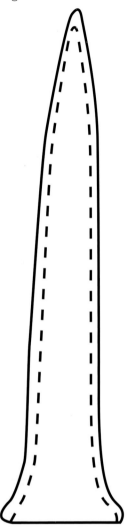

Fig. 1 - Stitching Diagram for Handle. Leave wide (bottom) end open for turning.

4. Create a mock flat fell seam by trimming the edge of one seam allowance to 1/8". Press remaining 3/8" seam edge over 1/8" seam allowance, trapping the shorter seam allowance between the 3/8" seam allowance and the bag. Apply a thin coat of leathercrafting cement to overlap area only and roll with a brayer to smooth. Let dry.

5. Turn to right side and machine stitch 1/4" from seam, going through the glued layers. Tie thread ends, adding a dot of glue to secure, and cut excess thread.

6. With right sides together, binder clip red suede bottom piece to sides, matching side seam of bag to dot on pattern. Machine stitch 3/8" from edge, removing clips as you stitch and easing corners as needed.

Fig. 2 - Stitching diagram for lining. Leave a 5" opening for turning.

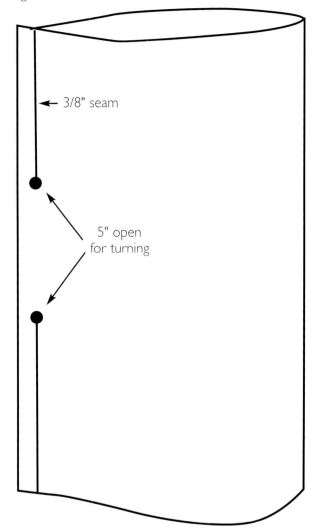

3/8" seam

5" open
for turning

7. Trim seam allowance on bag side of seam so that, when turned right side out, the seam from the bottom piece will easily cover the shorter seam allowance without causing puckering.

8. Glue vegetable tanned leather piece inside bag bottom.

Make & Attach Handles:

1. Binder clip two red suede handle pieces with right sides together. Stitch handles, beginning at wide end and stitching to narrow end using a 1/4" seam allowance. Backstitch, trim threads, and repeat for opposite side of same handle. Leave bottom edge open for turning (Fig. 1). Repeat to stitch the remaining two handle pieces.

2. Turn right side out. TIP: Use a 1/4" dowel to help. Once started, dowel can be inserted into inside of the suede to help gently push right sides out.

3. Press handles flat. Machine stitch close to seam (about 1/8" from edge).

4. Position handles and clip on opposite sides of tote, using bottom of bag and project photo as a guide. Machine stitch 1/8" from edge to secure and tie thread ends.

Add Lining:

1. Press iron-on interfacing on bag and bottom pieces of lining fabric. Fold 12" ends of bag liner in half, right sides together, and pin to hold in place.

2. Thread sewing machine with black thread and change needle to size 11. Beginning at the top, stitch 3/8" from edge as shown in Fig. 2, leaving a 5" opening. Backstitch ends to secure. Press seam flat.

3. With right sides together, pin bag lining to bottom lining piece, centering the side seam on one long edge. Stitch together, using a 3/8" seam allowance. Press seam allowances toward side edges of bag. Turn right side out and machine stitch 1/8" from seam to hold pressed seam in place. Trim seam allowances.

4. Attach magnetic clasp to right side of lining near center, measuring 1-1/2" from top edge. Use a craft knife to cut slits for the wings. Fold wings to center of clasp on back side of liner.

5. With right sides together, binder clip suede bag to lining along top edge, making sure that handles are positioned between the two layers. Machine stitch, first 3/8" from edge, then 1/4" from edge to reinforce.

6. Turn right side out through opening in lining.

7. Press flat, and then topstitch 1/4" from seam.

8. Handstitch opening in lining to close.

Finish:

1. Thread sewing needle with red thread. Handstitch red fibers or yarns over topstitching at top.

2. Adhere short lengths of fuzzy gimp braid along the tops of the stamped face images using fabric adhesive.

3. Knot handles. ❑

SUPPLIES

Leather:

Aqua velvet pig suede
  2 squares, each 12" (front and back)
  3" x 25" (gusset)
White kidskin leather - 8 pieces, 1-1/4" x 4"
White suede lacing, 1/8"

Other Supplies:

Stencil
Acrylic craft paint - White
Textile medium
Round bamboo handles, 7-1/2" diameter
1/2 yd. white cotton blend fabric (for lining)
1/2 yd. iron-on interfacing
White polyester blend thread
Poster board
Spray adhesive
6 white pony beads
16 aqua eyelets, size: 1/8"
White glue

Tools:

Ink pen
Disappearing ink pen (or pencil)
Leather shears
Binder clips
Straight pins
1/8" drive punch
Poly punch board
Foam plate
Cosmetic sponge
Wet wipes
Paper towel
Sewing machine with needle sizes 11 and 18 (or applicable needle size for your machine)
Sewing needle
Iron
Ironing board
Toothpick

STENCILED SUEDE HANDBAG

With the wide array of stencils on the market, there is no end to the stylish prints you can apply to soft pig suede. Here, the aqua color scheme and bamboo handles provide a summery, tropical look.

INSTRUCTIONS

Cut & Punch:

1. Photocopy handbag pattern-punch template and enlarge 200%. Trace or photocopy strap pattern-punch template. Attach patterns to poster board using spray adhesive. Cut out.

2. Use disappearing ink pen to trace handbag pattern on back side of aqua suede squares. Make a small dot on the back of each piece to mark the location of slash marks. Cut out, using leather shears.

3. Working one piece at a time, place the pattern on top of the cut suede piece and binder clip to hold in place. Use 1/8" drive punch, mallet, and punch board to punch the strap attachment holes.

4. Use pattern-punch template to cut eight straps from white goatskin pieces.

5. Punch lacing holes, using the 1/8" drive punch, punch board, and mallet. Set aside.

6. Pin handbag pattern to a double layer of lining fabric. Cut out the two pieces needed using scissors. Use straight pins to mark location of slash marks found on pattern on each piece.

7. Cut a 3" x 25" strip of lining fabric for the gusset lining.

8. Using the same pattern pieces, cut out iron-on interfacing.

Stencil:

1. Pour a small amount of white paint on a foam plate or palette and mix with an equal amount of textile medium.

2. Dip cosmetic sponge in paint mixture, daub off excess, and stencil the front sides of the front and back handbag pieces, using a pouncing motion. Reload sponge as needed. (Gusset is not stenciled.) (Photo 1) Let dry.

   • For best results, clean stencil with a wet wipe and dry with a paper towel before repositioning to stencil another area.

   • For added dimension, apply a slightly heavier coat of paint to some stenciled areas.

Continued on page 64

continued from page 62

Sew:

Slash marks at upper side edges of handbag pattern indicate starting and stopping points of gusset.

1. With right sides together, matching edges, use slash marks as a guide to binder clip one 25" side edge of suede gusset to a suede handbag piece. (Photo 2)

2. Thread sewing machine equipped with a size 18 sewing needle with white thread. Machine stitch the gusset and handbag piece together, stitching 3/8" from edge and removing binder clips as you stitch. Tie thread ends in a square knot. Use a toothpick to add a small drop of glue to knot to secure.

3. Trim gusset seam allowance only to 1/8". Press both seam allowances toward gusset. Topstitch close to seam.

4. With right sides together, binder clip remaining suede handbag piece to opposite side of gusset and stitch as you did the first previous side, stitching the same direction. (This prevents rippling.) Tie thread ends, add a dot of glue to secure, and trim thread.

5. Follow manufacturers' directions to iron interfacing to back sides of all three lining pieces.

6. Using straight pins, stitch one side lining piece to lining gusset piece, backstitching as needed to secure thread ends.

7. Place handbag pattern on remaining fabric lining piece. Use the disappearing ink pen to make dots at bottom of the lining piece that correspond to those on pattern. Remove pattern.

8. Leaving the area between the marked dots unstitched, stitch remaining side edge of gusset to lining . Do not trim seam allowance on unstitched area. (This part of the liner will be handstitched after turning.) Backstitch as needed to secure thread ends, and trim excess.

9. Position suede inside fabric liner with right sides together. Binder clip to hold in place along top edges of handbag and on gusset ends.

10. Machine stitch handbag pieces together, stitching 3/8" from edge. Tie thread ends in a square knot and add a drop of glue to secure ends.

11. Trim suede seam allowance to 1/8". Clip both suede and fabric corners and curves to ease. Turn right side out through opening in liner.

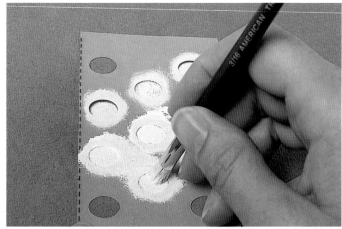

Photo 1 - Stenciling one of the suede handbag pieces.

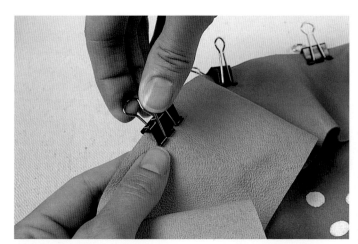

Photo 2 - Clipping the gusset to a handbag piece with binder clips.

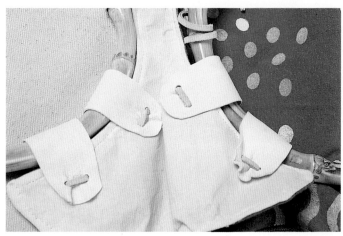

Photo 3 - The handbag attachment straps, shown from the inside.

12. Press top edges flat, then topstitch 1/4" from edge. Use needle and thread to whipstitch liner closed.

Install Eyelets:

1. Suede side up, place open purse on a punch board. Using the holes previously punched around top edge of suede as a guide, punch through lining fabric on back side with 1/8" drive punch and mallet. Repeat to punch all remaining holes.

2. With suede side up, working one eyelet at a time, insert 1/8" eyelets through punched holes, going through both suede and lining layers, then set with eyelet setter and mallet.

Connect Handbag to Handles:

1. Cut an 18" length of 1/8" white suede lace and tie an over-hand knot in one end. Fold goatskin attachment strap over bamboo handle ring. Center strap holes over one set of eyelets on handbag. Slip loose end of suede lace through strap hole, eyelet, and corresponding strap hole on opposite side. Pull taut, then bring lace end back to front side of handbag through second set of holes. Tie an overhand knot to secure. Cut excess. Repeat as needed to attach remaining straps to handles. (Photo 3)

2. Cut a 12" length of 1/8" white lace. Tie an overhand knot. Slide six white pony beads on the lace and knot the remaining end.

3. Divide beads, pushing three to each knotted end. Bring ends together to create a loop. Slip loop under bamboo ring at center front of handbag. Bring the beaded ends through the loop and pull to cinch in place on ring. ❏

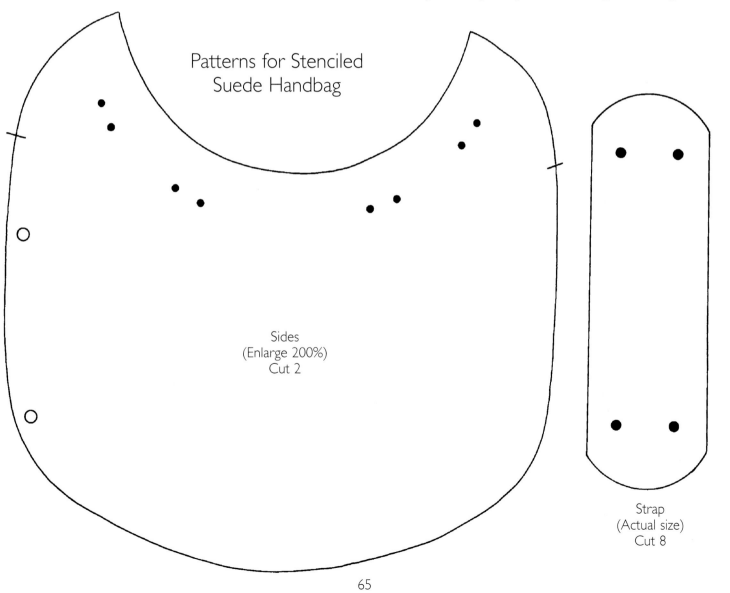

Patterns for Stenciled
Suede Handbag

Sides
(Enlarge 200%)
Cut 2

Strap
(Actual size)
Cut 8

CELL PHONE POUCH

Made from small pieces of leather, this functional project makes a great gift. You can adjust the length and width of the bag as needed to fit your (or someone else's) cell phone, and then top it off with this filigree punched leather flap.

SUPPLIES

Leather:

Tan deer-tanned cowhide
  2 pieces, 4" x 6-7/8" (bag)
  1 piece, 3" x 5-1/4" (flap)
Black doe kidskin, 3" x 5-1/4"
48" black latigo lacing, 1/8"

Other Supplies:

75" black waxed thread
35" black sewing awl thread
Leather sheen finish
Poster board
Spray adhesive

Tools:

Binder clips
Decorative filigree drive punches
  - tear drop shape, pie shape
Round hole drive punches -
  5/64", 1/8"
Mallet
Poly punch board
Large eye needle
Small glover's needle
Rotary hand sewing punch *or*
  stitching awl
Leather shears
Scissors
Needlenose pliers

INSTRUCTIONS

Cut & Punch:

1. Photocopy pattern with punch templates. Attach to poster board using spray adhesive. Cut out with scissors.

2. Binder clip flap pattern with punch template to face side of black kidskin piece. Cut out using leather shears. TIP: For best results, reposition clips as needed to keep pattern in close contact with the flap as you cut away excess leather.

3. Place the black flap, template attached, on the punch board. Use the mallet with the 5/64" round hole, tear drop shape, and pie shape drive punches to punch the design on the flap. Remove punch template.

4. Binder clip flap pattern to back side of 3" x 5-1/4" tan leather piece. Cut out using leather shears.

5. With back sides together, place black flap on tan flap. Place punch template on top of the black flap and binder clip together to hold in place. Use hand punch set to smallest setting or stitching awl and punch board to punch stitching holes around perimeter of flap, going through poster board and both leather layers. Set aside.

6. Binder clip bag pattern with punch template on face side of one 4" x 6-7/8" tan bag piece. Using the pattern as a guide, use hand punch set on second setting (or stitching awl and punch board) to punch those holes shown in red.

7. With back sides of tan leather bag pieces together, binder clip pattern with punch template on top. Punch all remaining stitching holes, going through template and both layers of leather. Use the 1/8" drive punch to punch the two larger holes at sides. Remove binder clips and pattern.

Construct:

1. Thread large eye needle with waxed thread. Tie an overhand knot in one loose end (but do not double thread). With right sides together, align punched holes and binder clip tan bag pieces together.

Continued on page 68

continued from page 66

2. Stitch, using the double back stitch method and keeping the thread pulled taut as you work. Begin at one upper corner, stitching in and out of the holes, working your way to opposite corner. At corner, return to starting point, bringing needle in and out of previously stitched holes as you work back to the starting point. Knot end, then whip-stitch a couple of times through existing holes to secure. Trim excess. See Fig. 1.

3. Turn bag right side out. Fold top edge over, aligning punched stitching holes and side seams. Binder clip to hold in place.

4. Thread needle with a single strand of waxed thread and tie an overhand knot at end. On back side of bag, beginning at full row of stitching holes along top edge of bag, bring needle up from between the folded layers, through center hole. Pull lightly to secure knot between the layers. Use punched stitching holes to stitch around top edge. When you reach the starting point, return to double back stitch to the starting point. Do not clip thread. See Fig. 2.

5. With black flap on top, position flap pieces on opposite sides of bag back, aligning stitching holes in all three leather pieces. (Photo 1 and Photo 2 show the placement of the flap on the bag.) Bring the threaded needle through back side of a corresponding hole in flap. Stitch bottom edges of flap to bag through bottom two rows of stitching holes. Double back, returning to starting point, and whip-stitch thread ends to secure between inside flap and bag layers. Trim thread ends. See Fig. 3.

6. Thread the glover's needle with a 35" strand of awl thread. Tie an overhand knot in end. Beginning at side edge of tan flap piece, bring needle through back side of hole nearest the previously stitched rows. Insert needle back through next flap hole, through punched hole in folded top edge of bag, and through black flap piece. Stitch side edges of flap to opposite side and return, backstitching to starting point. Whipstitch to secure ends. Cut excess thread.

7. Beginning on back side of bag, slip ends of latigo lace through holes in back and front of bag. Knot on front side to secure strap. ❏

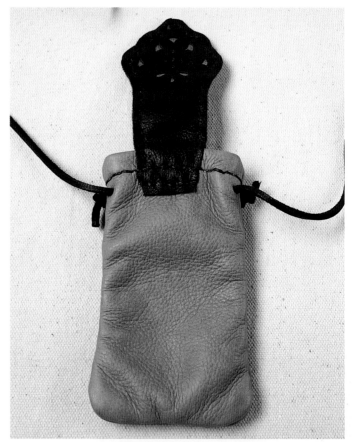

Photo 1 - The bag flap attached to the outside back of the bag.

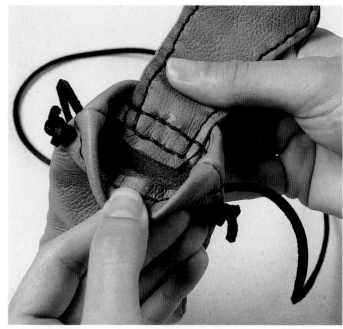

Photo 2 - The bag flap attached on the inside back of the bag.

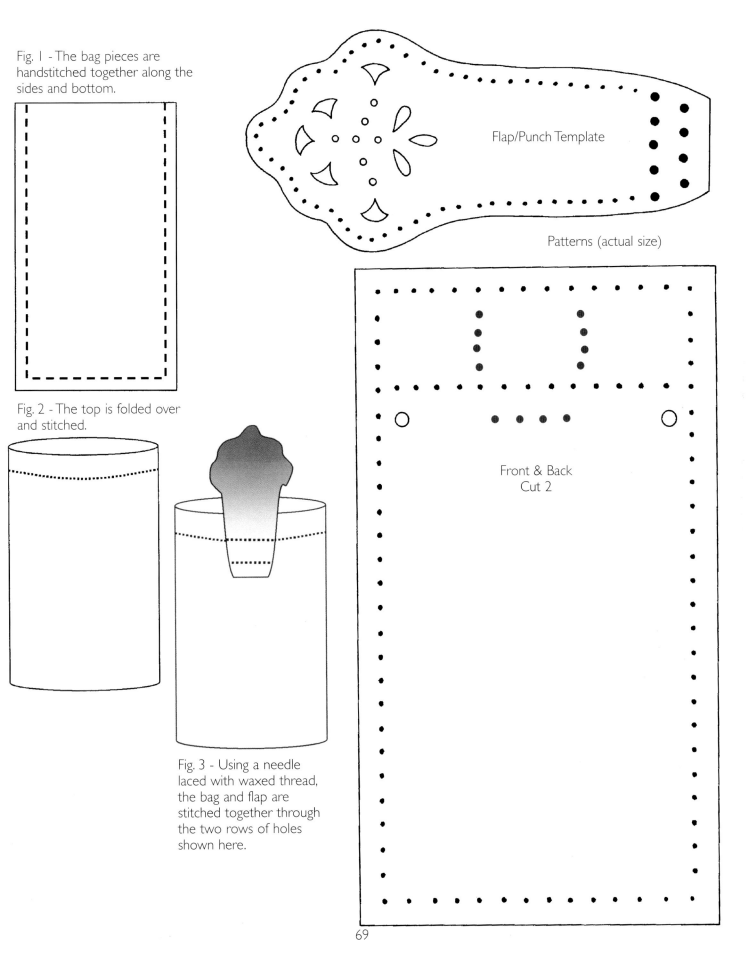

Fig. 1 - The bag pieces are handstitched together along the sides and bottom.

Flap/Punch Template

Patterns (actual size)

Fig. 2 - The top is folded over and stitched.

Front & Back
Cut 2

Fig. 3 - Using a needle laced with waxed thread, the bag and flap are stitched together through the two rows of holes shown here.

SUPPLIES

Leather:

Pewter velvet pig suede,
7" x 8-1/2"

Other Supplies:

Pewter or silver satinette fabric,
7" x 8-1/2" (lining)

White medium-weight fabric
interfacing, 7" x 8-1/2"

Pewter or silver polyester blend
thread

Metallic silver embroidery floss

19 strand bead stringing wire,
32"

2 silver C-crimps with looped
strap attachment

2 silver crimp beads

Crystal clear and silver lined
beads - seed, E, assorted shapes
and sizes

Seed beads - Black, silver

White beading thread

Poster board

Spray adhesive

Permanent fabric glue

Tools:

Leather shears

Scissors

Beading needle

Small eye embroidery needle

Sewing machine with size 18 and
size 11 needles (or applicable
size needles for your machine)

Toothpick

Binder clips

Crimping pliers

Bead tray (or small foam plate)

Ink pen

Optional: Handstitching punch *or*
scratch awl and punch board

BEADED EYEGLASS
PENDANT

Beads and flowers embroidered with metallic silver thread transform a
small piece of velvet pig suede into a useful, eye-catching pendant.

INSTRUCTIONS

Cut:

1. Make two photocopies of pattern. Attach one copy to poster board using spray adhesive. Cut out with scissors. Place on back of pewter suede piece and trace edges, using an ink pen. Cut out using leather shears.
2. Cut out remaining pattern. Pin on interfacing and cut out. Remove pattern. Trim 1/8" from scalloped bottom edge of bag.
3. Matching top edges, follow manufacturer's instructions to apply interfacing to back of pewter suede piece.
4. Cut same paper pattern along dashed line and discard scalloped bottom edge of pattern. Pin top portion on satinette lining. Cut out with scissors. Remove pattern.

Continued on page 72

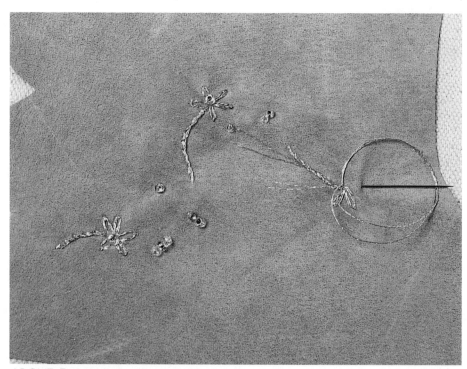

ABOVE: Embroidering the leather.

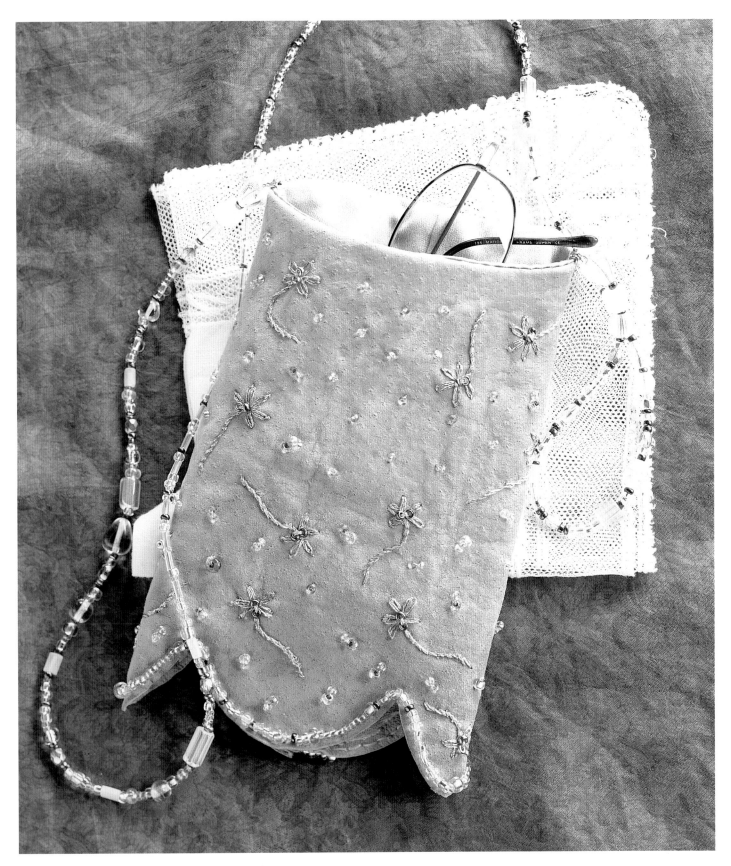

continued from page 70

Decorate:

1. Thread small-eye embroidery needle with two strands of silver embroidery floss approximately 24" long. Pull strands through needle about 5". Tie an overhand knot with longest ends to secure.

2. Beginning on back side of suede, pull needle through to top side so knotted ends are concealed on back. Without cutting threads, randomly embroider stem (Fig. 1), flower (Fig. 2), and bead accents over suede surface. Stitch one or two seed beads at centers of daisies. Daisies should appear to be floating with stems coming from various sides and angles. Whipstitch at thread ends to secure stitching. Cut excess, then repeat as needed. Don't stitch close to the edges; leave space for machine stitching.

Construct:

1. With right sides together, binder clip side edges of suede bag. Thread sewing machine and size 18 needle with pewter or silver thread. Machine stitch 3/8" from edge, removing binder clips as you stitch. **Do not** back stitch. Tie thread ends in a square knot. Add a tiny dot of glue to knot to secure. Trim ends.

2. Pin side edges of lining piece with wrong sides together. Change sewing machine needle to size 11 and machine stitch 1/4" from edge, backstitching at ends. Zigzag along 1/4" edge, back stitch, then cut excess. Turn right side out and press seam to one side.

3. Center stitched seam along bottom edge of lining, pin to hold in place, and stitch 1/4" from bottom edge.

4. With right sides together, binder clip top edges of suede to lining. Change sewing needle to size 18. Machine stitch 1/4" from edge. Turn suede right side out, inserting lining in center. Press seam around top edge flat.

Finish:

1. Thread a beading needle with 40" of white beading thread. Bring ends together and tie an overhand knot. Whipstitch twice on back side of suede seam allowance, then insert needle through to top side of suede at edge of seam. Slip assorted beads on the beading thread, creating a long strand.

2. Thread the glover's needle with 40" of beading thread. Bring ends together and knot. Slip needle through back side of suede approximately 1/8" from seam. With bead strand positioned 1/8" from bottom edge of bag, cross second strand of thread over beaded strand and return the glover's needle through the same hole. Repeat, stitching 1/8" from previous stitching hole as you work your way around bottom edge, attaching the bead strand and adding more beads as needed. Once back at starting point, whipstitch a few times on back side of bag with each needle to secure. Cut excess thread. TIP: For easy hand-stitching through velvet suede, use rotary hand sewing punch set to smallest dial setting to punch a row of stitching holes 1/8" apart and 1/8" from bottom edge.

3. Slip two silver crimp beads on jewelry wire 1" from end. Slip on a C-crimp and return same wire end back through silver crimp beads. Use crimping pliers to flatten crimp beads, holding the C-crimp in the looped section of the wire.

4. Slide assorted beads on wire to create a strand of the desired length. Slip on two more crimp beads, then C-crimp. Bring wire end back through the two round crimp beads and a few beads on the wire. Pull to adjust the loop, holding the C-crimp. Use crimping pliers to flatten round crimp beads.

5. Attach beaded strand to sides of bag. Use flat nose pliers to flatten the C-crimp over the top edge of the bag. ❏

Fig. 1 - Stem stitch

Fig. 2 - Lazy daisy stitch for flowers

Pattern for Beaded Eyeglass Pendant

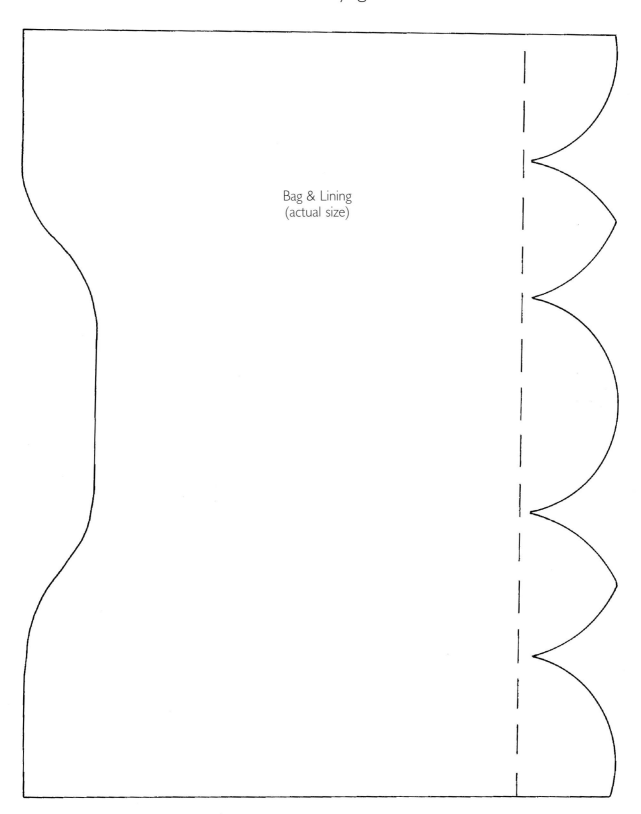

Bag & Lining
(actual size)

SUEDE HIP PURSE

This purse and the one that follows were created from the same basic pattern – changes in the type of leather and embellishments create two different looks. You can also enlarge the pattern to create a larger shoulder bag version.

Small velvet pig suede trim pieces are available in an assortment of colors and offer a good alternative to purchasing several full hides to make a small purse. Have fun mixing and matching colors to create this lightweight suede purse with a covered button accent on the flap. A piece of vegetable-tanned leather helps the lightweight suede hold its shape and allows easy access.

SUPPLIES

Leather:

Aqua, purple, and gold velvet pig suede trim pieces, each 3-5/8" x 9"

48" natural 2mm round lacing

Vegetable tanned leather, 3-1/2" x 4"

Other Supplies:

7/8" (2.2 cm) covered button and covering kit

Metallic acrylic paint - Sunset gold

Cosmetic sponge

2 brass eyelets with liners, 1/8"

18 gauge copper wire

Leather cement

Aqua, purple, and gold polyester blend thread

Gold embroidery floss

Card stock or index card, 1" x 3"

Poster board

Spray adhesive

Tools:

Sewing machine with size 18 needle (or correct size needle for your machine)

Embroidery needle

Rotary handstitching punch or scratch awl and 5/64" round hole drive punch

1/8" eyelet setting tool

Mallet

Poly punching board

Rotary cutter

Cutting mat

Clear acrylic ruler

Iron and ironing board

Dressmaker's chalk wheel

Roundnose jewelry pliers

Flatnose pliers

Wire cutters

Scissors

Instructions begin on page 76.

continued from page 74

INSTRUCTIONS

Cut:

1. Photocopy the patterns on pages 80 and 81. Attach to poster board using spray adhesive. Cut out.

2. Binder clip patterns to velvet pig suede pieces as indicated. Use a rotary cutter, cutting mat, and clear acrylic ruler to cut out the following pieces:

   From gold suede, cut the one-piece back

   From aqua suede, cut bag front and flap accent pieces

   From purple suede, cut two pieces, each 1" x 6-1/2", for gussets and a 1" x 4" accent strip for front

TIP: For best results and a cleaner cut, use clear acrylic ruler as a straight edge to cut along pattern lines.

Construct:

1. Following button covering kit manufacturer's instructions, cut a purple suede piece to cover button. Cover button as directed, then set aside.

2. Position aqua flap accent on gold suede flap, centering it. Glue about 1/4" from the flap edge, using a small strip of card stock to apply a thin layer of leather crafting cement. Let dry.

3. Thread sewing machine with aqua thread; thread bobbin with gold thread. With aqua side up, topstitch the aqua suede piece to secure, stitching 1/8" from edge. Tie threads on inside and trim.

4. Overlap short ends of purple gusset pieces by 1/2". Thread sewing machine with purple thread and make two lines of machine stitching, going through both suede layers. Tie thread ends on back and trim.

5. Use the 1" x 3" piece of card stock to spread a thin layer of leathercrafting cement on the back of the 1" x 4" purple suede strip. Apply at center of aqua bag front. Let dry.

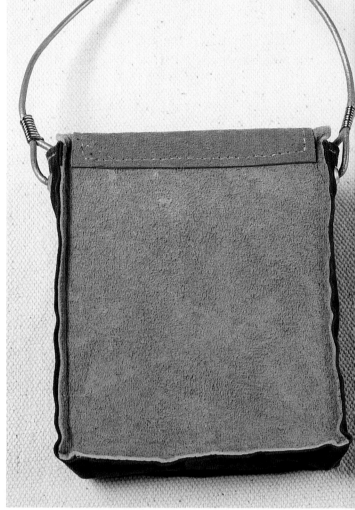

Photo 1 - Back view

6. Topstitch long side edges, using sewing machine with purple thread. Tie threads on inside and trim.

7. With back sides of suede together, binder clip gusset to bag front, matching side edges. Thread sewing machine needle with aqua and bobbin with purple thread. With aqua suede front piece on top, machine stitch the side edges 1/8" from the edge, easing at corners as needed. Remove binder clips as you stitch. Tie thread ends on back side and trim.

8. Turn top edge over 1/4" and press with iron to create a reinforced hem at the opening. Apply a thin layer of cement at the fold and finger press to hold until cement sets. Let dry.

9. With aqua piece facing you, machine stitch 1/8" from edge. Tie thread ends on back and trim.

10. Attach eyelets for the round lace strap by placing top edges of gusset on a punch board. Use 1/8" round hole drive punch to punch an eyelet hole 3/8" from top edge at center of 1" width. Repeat on opposite side.

11. One at a time insert eyelets through front of gusset, slip liner on back side, and set eyelets. See Photo 2.

12. Place the aqua bag front piece face side down on the back of the gold back-and-flap piece, aligning bottom edges. Use dressmaker's chalk to mark top edge of aqua piece on the gold.

Eyelet at side of purse

13. Binder clip back of purple gusset to back side of back and flap piece beginning at chalked line. Binder clip remaining edges as you work your way around the gusset to opposite side.

14. Thread sewing machine and needle with gold thread; thread bobbin with purple thread. With right side of gold suede piece facing you, machine stitch gusset to bag back 1/8" from edge. Knot thread ends and trim threads.

15. Apply a thin layer of cement to back of vegetable-tanned leather piece. Glue to back of gold suede on inside of bag.

Finish:

1. Determine button location on flap, using the pattern dot as a reference point. With rotary handstitching punch set on smallest setting (or scratch awl and punch board), punch two holes.

2. Thread embroidery needle with gold floss. Stitch button to flap through punched holes. Whipstitch on back side and trim ends.

3. Use rotary hand punch (or 5/64" drive punch, punch board, and mallet) to punch a series of small holes around outer edges of flap.

4. Dip a make-up sponge in sunset gold metallic paint. Wrap end around natural round lace and pull to paint the lace. Repeat as needed to coat completely. Let dry.

5. Beginning on outside of purse, slip the painted round lace strap through eyelet at side of purse approximately 2". Bring lace edges together to create looped attachment. Beginning 1/4" from top edge of suede, wrap 18 gauge copper wire tightly around both lace pieces. Cut wire with wire cutters and use round nose jewelry pliers to curl wire ends; positioning them between the two sides of lace. Use flat nose pliers to flatten wire, crimping it tightly to hold lace ends secure. Repeat for opposite side of strap. ❏

See patterns on pages 80 and 81.

SUPPLIES

Leather:

2-3 oz. vegetable-tanned leather:

   7-3/4" x 3-5/8" (back and flap)

   4" x 3-5/8" (front)

   1" x 12-1/4" (gusset)

1/8" black Latigo lacing, 48" length

2mm black round lacing, 12"

Other Supplies:

5 black acrylic beads, 1/2"

Metal spacer bead

Sheep's wool scrap

Soft cloth or clean kitchen sponge

Scrap paper

2 lengths black waxed thread,
   each 50"

Poster board

Spray adhesive

Ink pen

Swirl eyelet shape or other decorative accent for flap, such as screw-backed concho or button

Leather dye - Buckskin

Leather finish

Tools:

Rotary handstitching punch *or* stitching awl

Round hole drive punches - 1/8", 5/32"

Mallet

Poly punching board

Binder clips

Pattern weights

Teardrop-shaped background stamping tool, size A888

Swivel knife

Eyelet setter

Rotary cutter

Cutting mat

Clear acrylic ruler

Dressmaker's chalk wheel

Scissors

Water basin

Rubber gloves

LACED LEATHER HIP PURSE

For a more traditional leather look, try your hand at simple tooling to create this handstitched bag from vegetable tanned leather. Worn over head and shoulder, resting at your hip, this purse is perfect for carrying only necessities when you want to travel light.

INSTRUCTIONS

Cut & Punch:

1. Photocopy patterns with punch guides. Attach to poster board with spray adhesive. Cut out.

2. Set flap accent pattern aside. Place leather pieces on a cutting board and position pattern pieces on top. Use pattern weights to hold in place. Position clear acrylic ruler along the straight pattern lines and cut out, using a rotary cutter.

3. Binder clip patterns with punch guides to top of each leather piece. Use rotary hand punch set to smallest setting (or stitching awl and punch board) to punch small stitching holes shown along edges of all three pieces, following punch guides.

4. Place bag front piece on punch board and punch two holes with drive punch and mallet, using 1/8" round hole drive punch.

5. Punch strap holes near 1/2" from each end of gusset at center. Remove patterns.

Construct:

1. Place bag back-and-flap piece on punch board, face up. Place flap accent pattern on leather, centering it 1/4" from flap edges. Position acrylic ruler along pattern edges and use swivel knife to cut the pattern outline into leather. **Do not** cut completely through. Remove pattern.

2. Dampen a clean soft cloth with water. Wipe over flap surface. Let set briefly, then use mallet and background stamp to decorate the edges.

Continued on page 80

continued from page 78

3. Put on gloves. Place all leather pieces on layers of scrap paper. Dampen surfaces with water, let set briefly. Use wool scrap to apply one to two coats of buckskin leather dye, allowing surfaces to dry between coats. Let dry completely.

4. Spray with finishing spray to seal and protect.

5. Binder clip gusset to bag front, matching punched holes. Thread glover's needle with 50" of waxed thread. Beginning at one upper corner, insert the threaded needle from back to front, pulling threads until a 1" tail is left. Trap tail between the bag and gusset layers and whipstitch a couple of times through the same hole to secure. Continue to whipstitch along side edge, trapping remaining tail between the layers as you go. Ease leather at corners. When at opposite side, stitch through last hole a couple of times, then thread loose end of thread between the leather layers 1". Pull thread taut and cut excess.

6. Knot one end of 2mm black round lace. Insert opposite end through hole on back side of bag front, return lace through second hole then pull to leave a small loop closure on front. Adjust as needed and tie a second knot on back side of bag front. TIP: Slip largest bead back and forth through the loop a few times to gauge size before cutting excess lace close to knot.

7. Binder clip bag front to gusset and stitch same as with first side of bag.

Finish:

1. Using the pattern markings as a guide, attach metal accent to flap front, following manufacturer's instructions.

2. Knot one end of remaining 2mm black round lace and insert through hole on back side of flap, pulling excess to front. Slip on a 1/2" black acrylic bead, followed by a metal spacer bead. Adjust as needed to close purse flap. Knot end to hold beads in place. Cut excess lace.

3. Knot 1/8" lace strap near each end. Slip on two beads on each side. Knot again. Slip the ends of the lace through the punched holes on the sides and knot inside the bag to secure. ❏

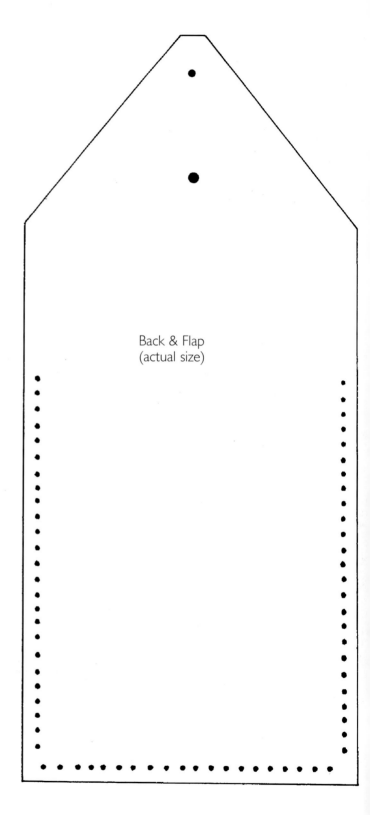

Back & Flap
(actual size)

Patterns for Suede Hip Purse and Laced Leather Hip Purse

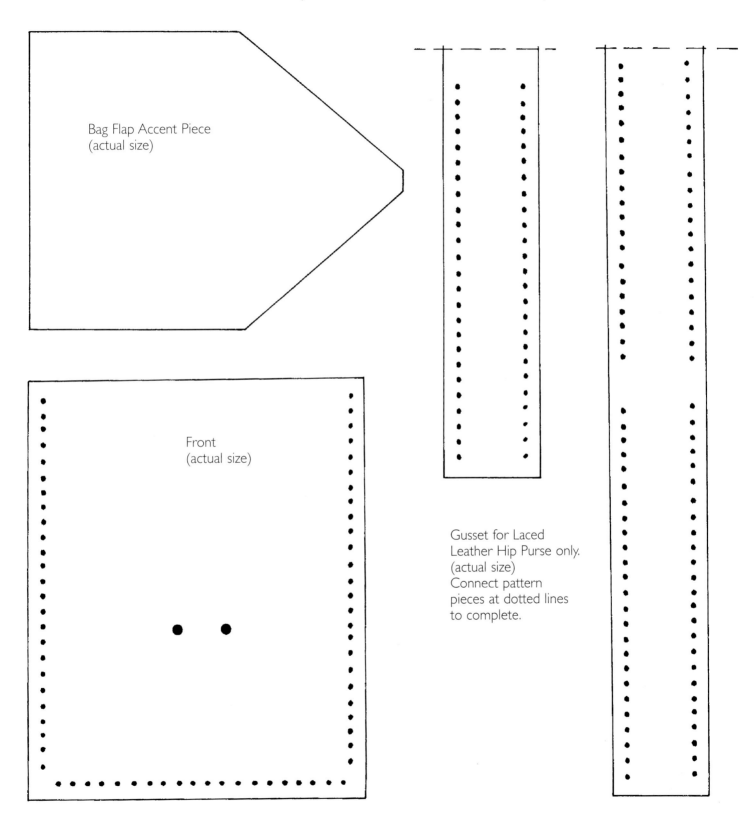

Bag Flap Accent Piece
(actual size)

Front
(actual size)

Gusset for Laced
Leather Hip Purse only.
(actual size)
Connect pattern
pieces at dotted lines
to complete.

ALLIGATOR-
GRAINED
HANDBAG

No one will believe you when you tell them that
the stylish handbag you made from scratch
started with an old hardback book!
The book cover provides the perfect backing
for this thin, grained cowhide. You can adjust the
pattern to suit the size of your book.

Instructions begin on page 84.

SUPPLIES

Leather:

Cordovan-toned embossed
  alligator grain cowhide split
  Bag - enough to cover book
  (see instructions)
  Straps - 2 strips, each 2" x 12"
  Closure - 2 strips, each 2-1/4"
  x 4"
Grained vinyl lacing

Other Supplies:

Old hardback book, size of choice
  (Mine was 5-5/8" x 8-3/4" and
  7/8" thick)
Black cotton blend lining fabric
Black thread
6 brass Chicago screws, 1/4"
Contact cement
Poster board
Brass oval clasp

Tools:

Craft knife
Pencil
Rotary cutter
Cutting mat
Clear acrylic ruler
Scissors
1-prong and 3-prong thonging
  chisels, size 1/8"
Round hole drive punch, 1/4"
Mallet
Poly punching board
2-prong lacing needle
1" metal brayer
Needlenose pliers
Electric drill press with 1/4" drill
  bit
Screw driver with flat end
Wood clamps
2 scraps birch plywood
Straight pins
Seam gauge
Iron and ironing board

INSTRUCTIONS

Prepare Book & Pattern:

1. Carefully use craft knife to cut inner pages from your book. (Photo 1) Remove the paper pages, leaving only the cover. (Photo 2)

2. Lay open book flat on poster board. Trace edges, marking spine. Use the ruler to measure, then mark a pencil line on poster board 1" beyond what will be the open top edge of hand bag, and 2-1/2" beyond each side. See Fig. 1. Remove book, place ruler along marked lines and draw lines to connect, creating a rectangular or square shape depending on the book you're using. Cut out poster board.

3. Along the spine marks, fold the back sides of poster board, matching outside edges. Place on cutting board.

4. Mark a line 1/2" from spine marks on both sides. With acrylic ruler positioned diagonally from top corner of poster board pattern to 1/2" from the spine edge, use rotary cutter to cut and remove a wedge shaped piece from each side. See Fig. 2. (This is the leather pattern for the handbag.)

Photo 1 - Using a craft knife to cut carefully along edges of book spine.

Fig. 1 - Book cover is positioned on poster board.

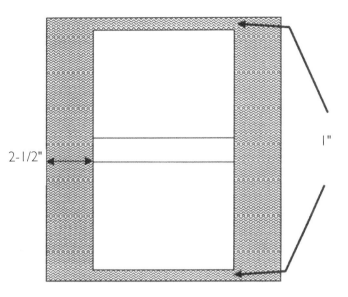

Photo 2 - Separating the book pages from the cover.

Fig. 2 - Cutting the poster board pattern.

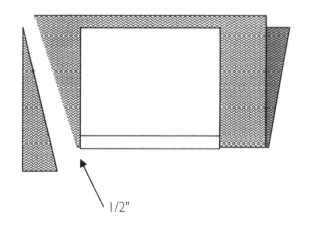

Cut & Construct:

1. Place pattern on back side of alligator grained cowhide and trace with ink pen. Mark spine location with dots. Using the rotary cutter, cutting mat, and straight edge acrylic ruler, cut out.

2. Center book cover on back side of leather, positioning spine at dots. Trace around outer edges of book on back side of leather, then remove. Clip side edges, cutting on either side of spine to book line. Repeat on opposite edge. See Fig. 3.

3. Apply contact cement to outside of book cover and back side of leather, coating only the area inside traced book lines. Let set briefly.

4. Adhere book cover to leather, matching outer edges of book with the previously traced lines. Smooth with palms to ensure good contact is made between surfaces.

5. Fold the 1" leather extension along top edge of handbag over the book edge. Draw a line to mark its location on inside of book cover and side edges of leather. Unfold. Apply contact cement to areas that will be inside the fold. Let set briefly, then fold the extension over book edge, pressing cement-coated areas together. Smooth with palms or brayer so that good contact is made. Repeat on opposite side. See Fig. 4. Clip corners to make side edges straight. See right side of Fig. 4. Let cement dry completely.

continued on next page

continued from page 85

6. Bring top edges of handbag together, with right sides of leather facing one another. Binder clip to hold in place. Measure to find center, then mark handle positions 2-1/2" on each side of center and 1/2" from top edge.

7. Place handbag between two scraps of birch plywood, position as needed for proper hole alignment, and drill through all layers using a 1/4" drill bit. (Handle holes on front and back should line up.)

8. Open handbag and lay flat. At center of what will be back side, drill two holes, 1-3/8" apart, 1/2" from top edge.

9. Attach swivel closure to front of handbag, centering it about 3/8" from top edge. Punch slits needed for closure wings, using single 1/8" thonging chisel. Attach swivel closure to front.

10. Fold book covers together and binder clip wrong sides of leather together at side edges. Place on punch board. With mallet and 3-prong 1/8" thonging chisel, punch a row of lacing holes approximately 3/8" from edge, going through both leather layers at the same time. (This will ensure lacing holes will line up.) Repeat on opposite side of purse. Reposition binder clips as needed, but do not remove them.

Stitch:

1. Thread a 2-pronged lacing needle with a piece of grained vinyl lacing that is 4 times the length of the side being stitched. Beginning at one upper corner, insert the threaded needle from back to front, pulling lacing through one slit at top, leaving a 1" tail. Trap tail between the bag layers and whipstitch a couple of times through the same hole to secure. Continue to whipstitch along side, trapping remaining tail between the layers as you go. At bottom, whipstitch twice through last slit, bringing needle between the two layers on second stitch. Weave the laced needle between the leather layers approximately 1", pull to outside edge and cut excess. Repeat on opposite side of handbag. If needed, use needlenose pliers to pull needle through lacing holes.

2. With back sides together, cement the flap pieces together. Use shears to cut corners, rounding them slightly.

3. With thonging chisels and punch board, punch a row of lacing slits around perimeter of flap. Insert a 50" length of

Fig. 3 - Position book cover on leather. Clip leather at center to both edges of book spine.

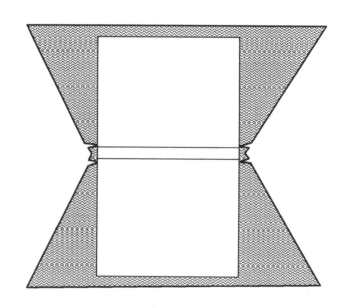

Fig. 4 - Fold the leather over the edges of the book cover and trim edges

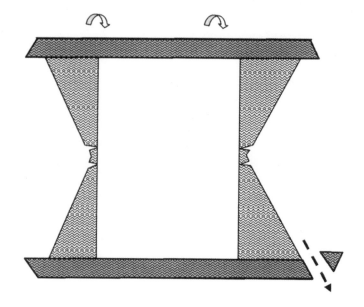

vinyl lace in the 2-pronged lacing needle and, beginning at center back of flap, whipstitch around flap, securing tail ends as you did on the sides.

Install Clasp:

1. With ink pen, mark opening for bag clasp 5/8" from center-bottom edge of flap front. Cut out the section, using a craft knife.

2. Use a 1/4" drive punch and mallet to punch two 1/4" holes corresponding to screw holes at center of purse back, 1/2" from edge on flap back.

3. Attach flap to back side of handbag with 1/4" Chicago screws. Tighten screw backs on inside with screwdriver.

Make Handles:

1. Use the clear acrylic ruler and an ink pen to draw a line lengthwise down the center on back side of each 2" x 12" leather strip. Apply contact cement to the entire back of each strip, let set briefly, and fold outer edges to center line. (Photo 3) Roll with brayer to ensure good contact is made between surfaces.

Photo 3 - Folding a handle strip to center line.

2. Measure 1/2" from each handle end and mark. Use a round hole drive punch and mallet to punch a 1/4" hole at center. Repeat on remaining handle.

Add Lining:

1. Use handbag pattern to cut lining.

2. Fold in half and stitch sides 3/8" from edge. Press seams to one side, then topstitch on right side close to seam.

3. Fold top edge over 1-1/2" and press. Machine stitch close to folded edge.

4. Determine position of lining on inside of handbag, making sure screw holes are not covered. On wrong side of lining, apply a 1" band of cement along top edge. Apply a second band of cement to inside of handbag where lining is to be attached. Let set briefly. Insert lining, with right side visible on inside of handbag. Press the cement-coated areas together.

Attach Handles:

Beginning on outside of bag, insert Chicago screws through bag and handle, attach screw on back, and tighten with screwdriver.

Repeat to attach remaining handle ends. ❏

SUPPLIES

Leather:
Cow suede, assorted colors
Orange suede
    Strap, 1-1/2" x 22"
    2 washer-like spacer pieces, 1/2"
    x 1-1/8"
2 red suede strap attachments,
    1-1/2" x 4"
Black doe kidskin, 10-1/2" x 5-1/2"

Other Supplies:
8 brass Chicago screws, 1/4"
2 pieces black faux leather 1/2"
    bias tape, 26" long
2 gold craft rings, 2"
2 pieces black fusible iron-on inter-
    facing, 9" x 12"
1 yd. black polyester blend fabric
    (lining)
Black quilting thread
Black polyester blend thread
60" grained vinyl lacing
Leathercrafting cement
Poster board
Spray adhesive
Brass magnetic bag clasp
Black foamcore board
White glue
Dressmaker's chalk

Tools:
Craft knife
Rotary cutter
Cutting mat
Clear acrylic ruler
Binder clips
Leather shears
Scissors
Sewing machine with size 11 and
    size 18 needles (or suitable sizes
    for your machine)
3-prong thonging chisel, size 1/8"
Round hole drive punch, 1/4"
Mallet
Poly punch board
2-prong lacing needle
Needlenose pliers
Straight pins
Seam gauge
Iron and ironing board
Flat blade screwdriver
1" metal brayer

PURSE OF MANY COLORS

Small cow suede squares left over from other projects are combined, patchwork-style, to create this stylish handbag. The kidskin bottom ensures it's both attractive and durable

Supplies pictured: suede squares, faux leather, bias tape, vinyl lacing.

Continued on page 90

INSTRUCTIONS

Cut:

1. Use the grid marks on the clear acrylic ruler to measure, then cut 24 suede pieces exactly 3" x 3" square with straight, smooth edges.
2. Cut a 19" x 25" panel of black fabric for lining.
3. Photocopy pattern for handbag bottom and cut out, following outer pattern line.
4. Pin pattern to lining fabric and cut out. Use dressmaker's chalk to mark dot along one side edge. Remove pattern.
5. Adhere pattern to poster board with spray adhesive. Cut out and binder clip to black kidskin leather. Cut out, using leather shears. On back side, use dressmaker's chalk to mark reference points at both side edges. Remove pattern.
6. Cut purse bottom pattern, following inside line. Trace pattern on foamcore board, then cut out using a sharp craft knife and cutting mat.

Assemble Suede Panel:

1. Place 12 suede squares side by side, face down, on ironing board, arranging them three squares tall by four squares wide in a color pattern of your choosing.
2. Place one 9" x 12" piece of fusible interfacing on top and press to attach.
3. Repeat steps 1 and 2, making a second set of 12 suede squares.
4. Thread sewing machine equipped with a size 18 needle with black quilting thread and set machine to widest zigzag setting. With suede panels right side up, zigzag stitch the 3" squares together, beginning at the edge of each row and sewing to opposite edge. Repeat for all rows and columns. Do not backstitch. Pull loose thread ends to back, tie a square knot, and trim ends. Add a drop of white glue to knots to secure.
5. Place panels side by side, matching one 9" (3 squares) edge and binder clip. Zigzag stitch to join, creating a panel three squares tall by eight squares wide.

Lace Seam:

1. Use a 3-prong chisel to punch lacing slits 1/4" from edge along each 9" end.
2. Thread a 2-prong lacing needle with vinyl lacing. Beginning on back side on one edge, insert needle and pull lacing to front, leaving a 2" tail. Take needle through first slit on opposite edge and pull lacing to back side. Insert needle through the first slit again and pull lacing through to front. Continue to second slit in opposite side edge. Repeat to whipstitch the two edges together, trapping the end of the lace between back of suede and stitches as you sew. Reinforce at corners by stitching an X-shape, then continue to bottom edge. Whipstitch once at bottom, going through one slit twice to bring lace to back. Thread

needle between stitches and back of suede about 2". Cut excess lace. TIP: Use a binder clip to hold the bottom edge together for easy stitching.

Add Bottom:

1. With right sides of leather and suede together, binder clip black kidskin bottom to bottom of the suede panel. TIP: For best results, center one 3" square of the side panel between the chalk marks at each end of bottom - the laced joint will be just off center. (Photo 1, Photo 2)
2. Machine stitch side panel to purse bottom, setting sewing machine to straight stitch 1/4" from edges. Tie thread ends. Secure with dots of glue.

Prepare Lining:

1. Change sewing machine needle to size 11 and thread machine with black sewing thread.
2. With right sides of fabric together, machine stitch 19" edges of side lining using a 1/2" seam allowance. Backstitch at ends and trim threads. Press seam flat. Fold in half to bring wrong sides of seam edges together. Press along fold line.
3. With wrong sides of seams pinched together, pin side lining of purse to bottom lining piece, matching the seam with marked dot on the bottom piece. Machine stitch 3/8" from edge, removing pins as you stitch. Press seams toward sides.

Photo 1 - Position laced seam off center.

Photo 2 - Placing the laced seam off center will ensure placement of one whole square at sides. This will hold purse open along bottom and prevent buckling during use.

Fig. 1 - Punching Guide for Strap Attachment (actual size)

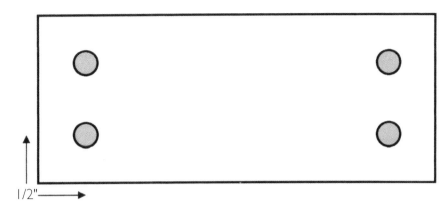

1/2"

Fig. 2 - Punching Guide for Strap (actual size)

3"

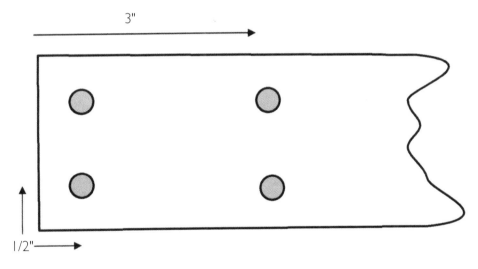

1/2"

4. Attach magnetic closure to inner lining, positioning one side of the magnetic piece over the seam 3/4" from top edge. Use a craft knife to cut slits for the wing portion of the closure. Slip on metal backing piece and close wings over backing. (When purse is completed, the back of the closure will be concealed between the lining and suede layers.) Attach remaining half of closure on opposite side.

Construct:

1. Insert foamcore in bottom of purse, positioning it to match bottom edge. *Option:* Use leathercrafting cement to hold it in place.

2. Insert lining in purse with wrong sides together, matching top edges. Use binder clips to hold together.

3. Using a size 18 needle in your machine, stitch suede and liner together 1/4" from top edge, removing binder clips as you stitch.

4. Place wrong sides of the two 26" faux leather bias tape pieces together. Leaving 1/2" from one end unstitched, machine stitch 1/8" from one edge. Backstitch to secure ends and trim thread.

Continued on next page

Continued from page 91

5. Beginning at the 1/2" that was not stitched together, open the two layers of bias tape. Leaving the 1/2" portion free, apply a thin layer of cement to inside edges of one small section of bias tape. Working one area at a time, slip the cement-coated bias tape over top of purse, starting at one side edge. Once back at the starting point, trim stitched end so the 1/2" unstitched end can be cemented on top, overlapping 1/2".

Attach Strap:

1. Use punch board, mallet, and 1/4" round hole drive punch to punch two holes 1/2" from edges on both ends of 1-1/2" x 4" attachment straps. See Fig. 1.

2. Open purse and place on punch board. Use one strap attachment as a guide to mark, then punch, two corresponding holes 1" from top edge of purse through both lining and suede layers. Repeat on opposite side.

3. Attach straps to purse using 1/4" Chicago screws with the 2" craft ring in the looped top edge. Tighten screw on inside of purse using screwdriver. Repeat to attach straps to both sides.

4. Using same punch, punch both ends of 1-1/2" x 22" strap, using Fig. 2 as a guide.

5. Punch corresponding holes in suede washers. (These add thickness needed to comfortably attach the Chicago screws.)

6. Loop one strap end through a 2" craft ring, insert a suede washer between the layers, insert a Chicago screw head through all layers and tighten screw on back side. Repeat to complete fastening of strap. ❑

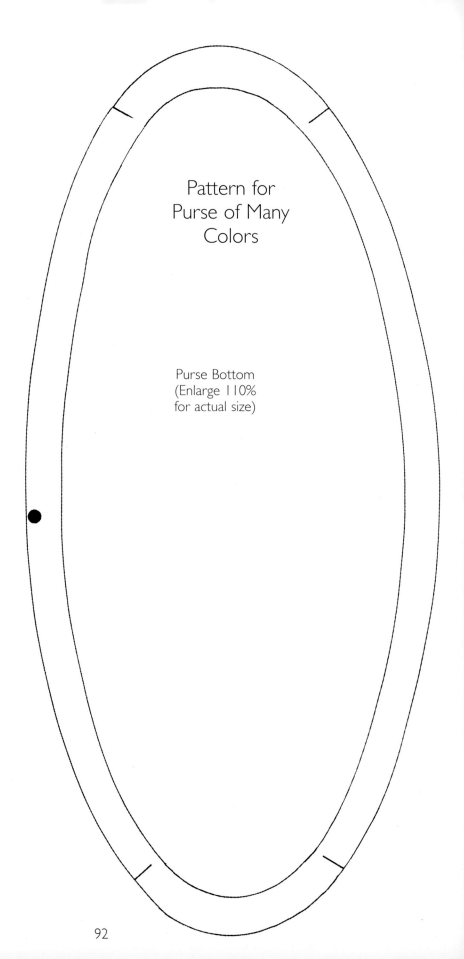

Pattern for
Purse of Many
Colors

Purse Bottom
(Enlarge 110%
for actual size)

Pattern for Gypsy Quilted Purse

Instructions begin on page 95.

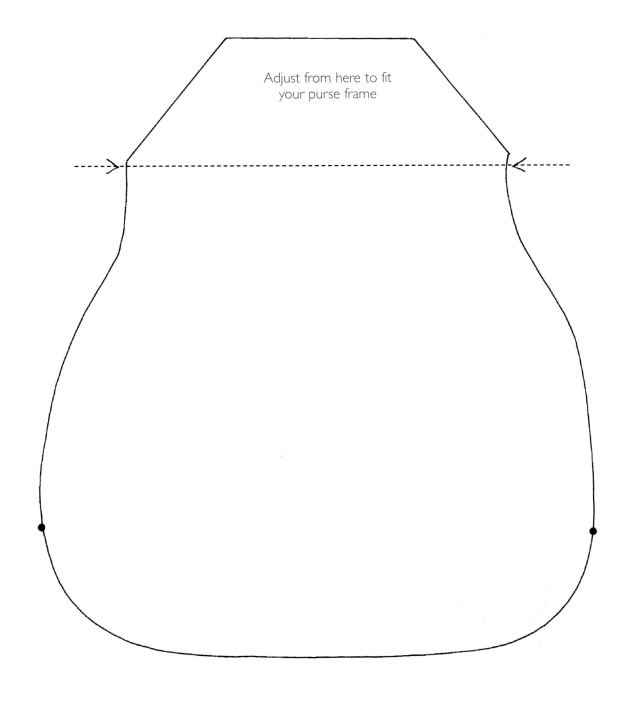

Adjust from here to fit
your purse frame

SUPPLIES

Leather:

Scraps of velvet pig suede, assorted colors

Other Supplies:

1/2 yd. crepe satin lining fabric

Cotton batting

Sewing thread to match lining fabric

Metallic embroidery floss, colors of choice

Polished Brass purse frame, 4-5/8" wide x 3-1/2" tall

18" gold finish chain

2 gold split rings, 10mm

Short lengths of trim, including plain, beaded, and gimp braid

Seed beads - Black, gold

Black beading thread

20" beaded trim

Solvent based inkpad - Black

Metallic acrylic paint - Sunset Gold

Tools:

Straight pins

Binder clips

Rotary hand sewing punch

Stitching awl

Poly punching board

Embroidery needle

Beading needle

Sewing machine with size 11 needle

Filigree drive punches, assorted shapes

5 rubber stamps, your choice of motifs

Cosmetic sponge

Foam plate

Scissors

GYPSY QUILTED PURSE

After working with leather for a while you'll begin to accumulate scraps left over from previous projects. Like a trip down memory lane, you can put your small scraps to use in this decorative little purse. Use it for special occasions or frame it as a wall accent in your bedroom or bath.

Pictured from top to bottom: lining fabric, embroidery floss, suede scraps, rubber stamps, purse frame, beaded trim.

Instructions begin on page 97

A number of embroidery stitches were used to decorate this purse on both sides, including the running stitch, blanket stitch, whipstitch, stem stitch, back stitch, and French knots. You can use any stitches you like or consult a book about embroidery for ideas.

This construction technique can easily be adapted to any metal purse frame. Many frames come with a purse pattern you can use as a template. Reduce or enlarge the pattern given to fit your frame.

INSTRUCTIONS

Stamp:

1. Stamp suede pieces with your favorite rubber stamps, using black ink.

2. Stamp some pieces with Sunset Gold - pour a small amount of the acrylic paint on a foam plate, dip cosmetic sponge in paint, daub off excess, and apply to stamp. Quickly stamp suede. Reapply paint as needed.

Punch:

Use the filigree punches and handstitching punch to create interesting designs on some suede pieces. (The lining fabric will show through the punched holes, adding to the decorative effect.)

Make the Underlining:

1. From lining fabric, cut four squares that are about 2" larger than your purse pattern for bag front and back and two 2-1/2" x 15" strips for bag bottom. (Note: size may vary depending upon your purse size.).

2. Photocopy purse pattern that comes with the frame or create your own purse pattern. Stack 7" crepe satin lining squares. Pin pattern on top and cut out, following pattern lines, to create four purse pieces. Set two pieces aside for the lining.

3. Cut two 8" squares and one 3-1/2" x 16" strip of cotton batting.

4. One at a time, with right sides up, use needle and thread to baste a crepe satin purse piece to each 8" square cotton batting piece. TIP: To prevent fraying, leave a 1/2" cotton border around all edges of the crepe pieces.

5. Attach one crepe satin purse bottom strip to the 3-1/2" x 16" piece of cotton batting.

Create & Stitch Purse Design:

1. Select suede pieces and position them on the purse pattern like pieces of a jigsaw puzzle. Cut the suede pieces as needed to align them within the pattern. Repeat the process to create the opposite side and the bottom strip.

2. To easily embroider edges, use a handstitching punch set on smallest punch setting (or a stitching awl and punch board) to punch stitching holes on the edges of all suede pieces. (You can punch additional holes later for stitching beads.)

3. Use a variety of embroidery stitches and floss colors to stitch together suede pieces and attach them to the padded lining fabric pieces for the purse front, back, and bottom. Leave some areas open to revealing the lining fabric or for trim pieces.

4. Use dots on the pattern as a reference as you hand baste the beaded trim along the bottom edge, stitching 3/8" from purse edge on the face side of the front and back. The beaded trim should dangle freely below the purse.

5. With right sides together, machine stitch one long edge of the purse bottom piece to one purse piece. Repeat to stitch opposite purse piece to remaining side of purse bottom. Use the arrows on the pattern as guides. Turn right side out.

6. Use a beading needle and thread to attach ropes of gold seed beads to purse front, crossing over side seams to tie the design together. Whipstitch bead ropes to purse to secure as you go, using a second needle and thread. Whipstitch thread ends at back and trim.

Add the Lining:

1. Machine stitch the lining pieces together.

2. With right sides together, stitch lining to purse, leaving a 4" opening at one side edge of lining for turning.

3. Turn and finger press the top edge flat.

Stitch to Frame:

1. Use black beading thread to handstitch purse to inside of the purse frame through the stitching holes. Whipstitch at ends and trim threads.

2. Stitch a row of gold beads to the frame, covering the black stitches.

3. Attach additional beaded accents to top edge of frame.

4. Attach the chain through holes in purse frame, using 10mm split rings. ❏

LEATHER-TRIMMED
TRAVEL TOTE

Pieces of stamped and tooled vegetable-tanned leather provide striking, useful accents on a fabric tote. You can sew the tote from my instructions or buy a plain tote and apply the leather pieces to it. Add an initial to personalize.

SUPPLIES

Leather:

4-5 oz. vegetable-tanned leather:

    2 pieces, 1-1/2" x 20" (top band)

    1 piece, 6" x 9" (pocket)

    1 piece, 4-3/8" x 2-1/2"
    (pocket accent)

Other Supplies:

Striped medium weight drapery fabric, 19" x 32"

Tapestry women's belt or patchwork strip of drapery fabrics,
    2-1/4" x 28"

Black polyester blend lining fabric, 19" x 32"

Fusible webbing (for applique),
    5-3/4" x 12"

Black sewing machine thread

Black sewing awl thread

Leather dye - Cordovan

Leathercrafting cement

Metallic acrylic paint - Sunset gold

Black foamcore, 5-3/4" x 12"

Satin sheen leather finish

Tools:

Sewing machine with size 11 needle (or applicable size needle for your machine)

Sewing needle

Alphabet template, 1-3/4"

Modeling spoon *or* craft stick

Spacer set for leather crafting with #5 overstitching wheel

3-in-1 bone folder/creaser/slicker

Stamping tools - Teardrop shaped background, decorative filigree accent

Mallet

Stone slab *or* poly punch board

Clear acrylic ruler

Stylus

Soft cloth

Sheep's wool scrap

Rubber gloves

Sponge

1" paintbrush

Craft knife

Scissors

Binder clips

Iron and ironing board

Optional: Stitching pony

Instructions begin on page 100.

continued from page 98

INSTRUCTIONS

Stamp the Bands:

1. Wipe the leather bands with a water-dampened sponge. Place clear acrylic ruler 1/4" from each edge and roll over-stitching wheel along edge of ruler to mark stitching holes shown at top, bottom, and ends.

2. On one end of each band, mark another row of over-stitching holes 1-1/2" from the end. (This is for the overlap found at center front and back.)

3. Place both bands on a punch board or covered stone slab. Beginning with end with the over-stitching holes, measure 3/4" and press a small dot in the leather with the pointed

Photo 2 - Rubbing the initial in the leather, using a plastic template.

end of a stylus. Continue from this point, pressing a series of barely visible dots into the leather, spacing them 1-1/2" apart along center of each band.

4. Case (dampen) leather again, if needed. Position filigree stamp, centering it on each dot, and stamp with a mallet. Hold the stamp upright as you stamp. Repeat on second band. (Photo 1)

Stamp the Pocket:

1. Case the leather pocket piece with a water dampened sponge. Impress stitching reference points 1/4" from all outside edges using the over-stitching wheel and ruler.

2. Beginning 3/4" from one corner, use the clear acrylic ruler and a stylus to mark reference dots for stamping filigree pattern 1-1/2" apart, 3/4" from top edge. Mark the entire pocket, positioning dots 1-1/2" apart in all directions, staggering them from row to row.

3. Stamp filigree pattern at each dot. Set aside.

Photo 1 - Stamping the band.

Stamp the Personalized Accent:

1. Case the 4-3/8" x 2-1/2" piece of leather. Place alphabet template face down on leather with chosen initial at center. Use a modeling spoon or craft stick to rub over the letter, impressing the image. Remove template. (Photo 2)

2. Depress initial in the leather using a teardrop-shaped background stamp to give a textured appearance, holding the stamp straight and striking firmly. TIP: For best results, move the teardrop shape along the side edge with the point coming toward you. (Photo 3)

3. Use the over-stitching wheel and ruler to mark stitching holes 1/8" from outside edges.

Example of the right and wrong way to fill in a design. Left shows correct way.

Dye & Antique:

1. Case leather with a water-dampened sponge. Place on a work surface covered with plastic or scrap paper. With gloved hands, use a sheep's wool scrap to apply one or two light coats of cordovan dye to the face side of all leather pieces. Keep the leather damp by resting it on a damp sponge. (Photo 4) Let dry.

2. Working with one piece at a time, quickly brush leather with a coat of sunset gold paint to antique. (Photo 5) **Do not** let paint dry on leather - wipe away excess immediately, leaving most of the color only in stamped areas. (Photo 6)

3. Use the side edge of the paint brush to add highlights along the edges of each piece. Let dry.

4. Apply leather finish. Set aside to dry completely.

Make the Tote:

1. With right sides together, fold tote fabric in half, bringing 19" top edges together. Pin along the side, then machine stitch both sides with coordinating thread, using a 3/8" seam allowance. Backstitch to secure stitching. Trim ends.

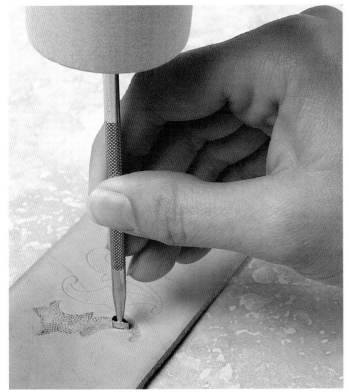

Photo 3 - Stamping inside edges of the initial.

Continued on next page

continued from page 101

2. Press side seams flat to one side. Use a ruler to measure 6" from bottom (folded). Mark with a straight pin. Fold bottom corner of bag up to the 6" mark, matching seams on inside. (Photo 7) Pin to hold in place and press along bottom and side edges of the triangle shaped piece.

3. Whipstitch to side of handbag at top point to hold in place. Turn right side out.

4. Machine stitch outer cover of tote to bottom of the triangular piece, creating box-like bottom of tote. (Photo 8)

5. Stitch the tote lining the same as the outside, but leave a 6" opening in one side seam.

6. With right sides together, pin top edge of lining to top edge of tote. Machine along top edge, using a 5/8" seam allowance. Backstitch at ends, trim threads, and turn right side out through side opening in lining.

7. Apply sticky-back fusible webbing to foamcore board, using an iron and following manufacturer's instructions. Peel off paper backing.

8. With sticky side down, insert through side opening of lining. Align with inside bottom corners of tote, turn over tote, and press bottom edge to adhere the board and fabric layers together.

9. Use a needle and thread to whipstitch side opening of lining.

10. Fold top edges of tote together; pinching at sides. With dressmaker's chalk and ruler, measure 4" from each side. Mark a dot 1" from top edge, on both sides of lining.

11. Using chalk mark as a reference, machine stitch one end of tapestry belt to front of tote, extending the belt 1" over front edge. Machine stitch to tote along tote's top edge and on all sides of the 1" extension. Stitch opposite end of belt to back side of tote.

12. Use 1/8" round hole drive punch, punch board, and mallet to punch snap holes at chalk marks, punching through all tote and handle layers on both sides. Attach snaps at 1/8" holes.

Photo 4 - Applying dye with a piece of sheep's wool.

Photo 5 - Brushing gold paint over leather to antique.

Assemble Tote:

Although not necessary to complete this project, a stitching pony is a helpful aid for handstitching leather pieces. With pieces held in position above the pony, both hands are free to quickly stitch along edges.

1. Following guide marks made with the over-stitching wheel, use stitching awl with black awl thread to hand-stitch leather bands around top edge of tote. Center band ends at front and back, overlapping them by 1-3/4", covering the ends of the strap. Whipstitch thread ends inside tote, using an embroidery needle.

2. Apply leathercrafting cement to back side of initial piece and adhere to center of pocket.

3. Handstitch around outer edges of piece, whipstitch ends on back, and cut thread.

Photo 7 - Folding side corner up to the straight pin located at 6" mark.

Photo 6 - Rubbing with a damp cloth to remove most of the paint.

Photo 8 - A finished corner.

4. Stitch top edge of pocket only, allowing enough thread to later stitch around entire pocket. Do not cut the awl thread ends.

5. Place pocket on the punch board and pierce each corner at one of the marked stitching holes using awl needle or stitching awl.

6. Place pocket on tote at center front. Thread an embroidery needle with sewing thread - any color will do. Whipstitch corners of pocket to tote to hold in place.

7. Handstitch sides and bottom of pocket to tote with stitching awl and thread. Whipstitch thread ends on back.

8. Remove thread at corners. ❑

DRAGONFLY GARDEN

SEED POUCH
&
TOOL TOTE

I'm an avid gardener, and it seems that I never have enough hands and pockets to carry all my "necessities" to and from the garden. You can use the pouch to carry and hold seed packets while planting - but don't pack it away, too soon! It's also terrific as a wall pocket for holding dried flowers or for collecting seeds from your favorite blooms for planting next season!

Made from sturdy vegetable tanned leather, the durable tool caddy is stamped with graceful dragonflies, leaves, and blooms. It's strong enough to carry small hand tools for gardening; filled with a silk or dried arrangement, it also makes an attractive centerpiece for the table.

The pouch and tote were stained with the same dye - one coat was applied to the pouch; two coats were applied to the tote, giving it a darker hue.

Instructions begin on page 106.

SUPPLIES

Leather:

2-3 oz. vegetable-tanned leather, 5-1/2" x 11"

40 " hunter green suede lacing, 1/8"

Other Supplies:

12 synthetic aged bone discs, 3/8" diameter

2 natural toned wooden beads, 1/2"

Buckskin dye

Antiquing finish for leather

Super sheen leather finish

Fine 4 oz. natural-tone artificial sinew

Tools:

Glover's needle

Modeling spoon

Spacer set for leather crafting with #6 over-stitching wheel

3-in-1 bone folder/creaser/slicker

Stamping tools - Teardrop-shaped background, size A888; seeder, size S706

Mallet

Round hole drive punch, 11/64"

Poly punching board

Clear acrylic ruler

Stylus

Soft cloth

Sheep's wool scrap

Rubber gloves

Scrap paper or plastic

Sponge

Swivel knife

Scissors

Binder clips

Stitching awl

Patterns are found on page 114.

DRAGONFLY GARDEN SEED POUCH

INSTRUCTIONS

Stamp & Tool:

1. Dampen the cut side edges of leather slightly with the sponge. Rub with the slicker until smooth.

2. Photocopy pattern.

3. Case the 5-1/2" x 11" leather piece with a water-dampened sponge. Let set briefly. Place pattern, printed side up, on face side of leather, positioning it at center 1" from top edge. Use a stylus to trace all pattern lines, including outer border. (Photo 1) Remove pattern. (Photo 2)

4. Carve stems and outer border lines into leather surface with swivel knife. **Do not** penetrate leather.

Continued on page 108

Photo 1 - Impressing the pattern on the leather with a stylus.

continued from page 106

5. Use teardrop-shaped background stamp to stamp tail and inside portions of all wings, leaving a thin line of unstamped leather between wings to separate. For tail, begin just under bottom wings and move stamp slightly with each strike, working your way down the tail, curving slightly as you near the end. (The teardrop shapes are visible on the tail, creating the segmented appearance.)

6. Use the seeder to stamp cone-shaped flowers at ends of stems and dragon-fly eyes.

7. Use the modeling spoon to smooth cut edges of stems. Create shading in and around leaves, stems, and drag-onfly by tilting the spoon slightly as you run along side edges, lightly compressing the cased leather.

Photo 2 - The pattern is transferred to the leather.

8. Use the point, sides, and/or rounded ends of teardrop shader to add additional texture and dimension in recessed areas.

9. Stamp a line of seeder dots along each pouch end.

10. Stamp random dots on other outside areas of pouch (Photo 3)

11. Beginning and ending 3/4" from each end, use the clear acrylic ruler and #6 over-stitching wheel to mark stitch-ing holes 1/4" from both side edges.

Stain & Antique:

1. Place leather on scrap piece of paper or plastic. Use a piece of sheep's wool to apply one or more coats of buckskin dye to face side of leather. Let dry.

2. Apply antiquing finish according to manufacturer's instructions. Let dry.

3. Apply leather sheen to seal and finish. Let dry.

Construct:

1. Place pouch on punch board, face side up. Use an awl to punch stitching holes along both side edges, but **don't** punch any holes along the folded bottom edge.

2. Fold pouch in half, bringing back sides together and matching holes at the top. Use your palms to press flat. Binder clip edges to hold in place while stitching.

3. Use a double-back stitch to stitch side edges together. Thread glover's needle with a 26" length of artificial sinew. Along one side edge, bring needle through back side of top hole, leaving a 1" tail. Whipstitch once through first two holes in both layers. Pull thread taut. Continue to stitch side edge, trapping the 1" tail between the leather layers as you go. At bottom, stitch over folded end and stitch your way back to top of pouch. Whipstitch twice at top, bringing

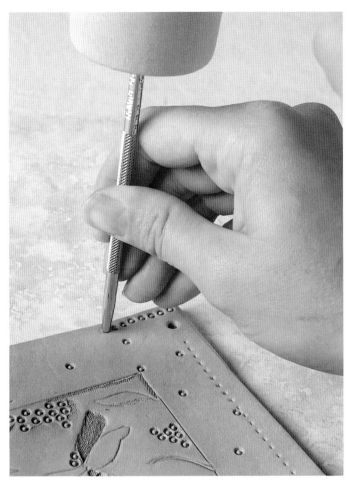

needle from between the leather layers with the last stitch. Weave needle in and out of stitching approximately 1" between the two layers. Trim thread ends.

4. Repeat to stitch opposite side.

5. Place on the punch board. Punch an 11/64" hole approximately 1/4" from each top corner, going through both leather layers.

6. Tie an overhand knot 6" from one end of 1/8" hunter green suede lace. Slide on three synthetic bone discs, a wooden bead, and three more discs. Tie a second overhand knot to hold in place. Slip lace end through hole in back side of pouch and tie an overhand knot at front.

7. Position lacing around neck to adjust to your desired hang length. Trim lace ends, if needed. Bead and attach remaining end of lace to pouch. ❑

Photo 3 - Stamping seeder dots along top edge.

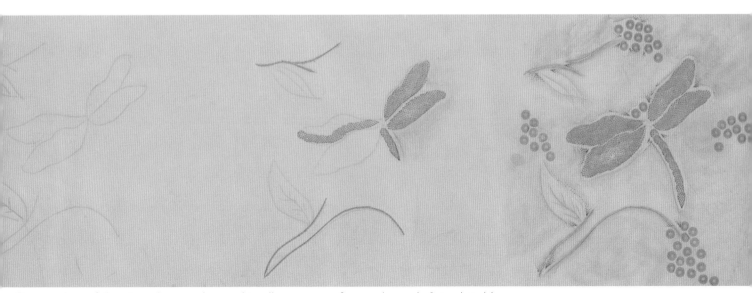

Progression of the stamping, carving, and tooling process for seed pouch & tool caddy.

SUPPLIES

Leather:

8-9 oz. vegetable-tanned leather
   1 piece, 14" x 27" (bottom)
   2 pieces, each 5" x 15" (handles)
Natural leather lacing, 1/8"
Dark brown grained lacing, 1/8"

Other Supplies:

Buckskin dye
Antiquing finish for leather
Super sheen leather finish
Acrylic craft paint - Burnt umber
Acrylic textile medium
Leather balm - Neutral
Poster board
Spray adhesive
Short length of string or yarn

Tools:

Paint brush, 1" flat
Leather shears
Craft knife
Cutting mat
3-in-1 bone folder/creaser/slicker
2-prong lacing needle
Modeling spoon
Spacer set for leather crafting
   with #6 over-stitching wheel
Stamping tools - Teardrop-shaped
   background, size A888, seeder,
   size S706
Mallet
Round hole drive punch, 11/64"
Poly punching board
Clear acrylic ruler
Stylus
Soft cloth
Sheep's wool scrap
Rubber gloves
Scrap paper or plastic
Sponge
Swivel knife
Binder clips

DRAGONFLY GARDEN TOOL TOTE

Stamp and tool a little or a lot to create this delightful, sturdy tote.

INSTRUCTIONS

Cut:

1. Photocopy patterns provided, enlarging as directed. Attach patterns to poster board using spray adhesive.

2. With leather face up on cutting board, position patterns and trace outer edges, using a stylus. Remove patterns.

3. Cut out pieces following pattern lines. TIP: For easy cutting, use an 11/64" round hole drive punch to punch rounded top edge of slits between the bottom four flaps. Insert craft knife in the hole, then cut to bottom of flap.

4. Replace patterns with punch templates on leather pieces and binder clip to hold in place. Place onto poly punch board and punch holes as shown, using an 11/64" round hole drive punch.

Apply Design:

1. Make four to five photocopies of leaf and dragonfly wing patterns. For a more realistic, dimensional effect, enlarge or reduce some copies to make a few different sizes. Cut to separate leaves from wings, leaving a small border.

2. Case top sides of all leather pieces with a water-dampened sponge.

3. Place dragonfly wing patterns **face up** on top of the leather piece. Trace with stylus. Reposition and trace in various positions on tote and at base of handle so that dragonflies appear to be flying. (Eyes and tails will be added later.)

   • **Do not** place photocopies face down on the dampened leather - this will cause ink to transfer to the leather, discoloring the surface permanently.

   • When a pattern begins to tear around the traced edges, discard it. Use a new one to prevent photocopy ink from discoloring leather.

Continued on page 112

continued from page 110

4. Use the swivel knife to cut curvy vine lines into leather in and around dragonflies, using the photo as a guide.

5. Position photocopied leaf patterns next to vine lines and trace with a stylus, repositioning as needed. Include several leaf sizes.

Stamp & Tool:

See the photos that accompany the Dragonfly Seed Pouch.

1. Use the teardrop-shaped background stamp to stamp inside portions of all wings, leaving a thin line of unstamped leather between the wings to separate.

2. Stamp the tail using the teardrop stamp. Begin just under bottom wings and move the stamp slightly with each strike, working your way down the tail and curving slightly as you near the end.

3. Use the seeder to stamp the dragonflies' eyes.

4. Use the seeder stamp to punch a cluster of small dots to create cone-shaped flowers on some vine ends.

5. Use the modeling spoon to smooth the cut edges of stems and create leaf lines. (You can see them easily on the leaf-shaped handle ends.) Create shading in and around leaves, stems, and dragonfly by tilting the spoon slightly as you run alongside the edges, lightly compressing the cased leather.

6. Use the point, sides, and/or rounded ends of the teardrop shader to add additional texture and dimension in recessed areas.

Stain & Antique:

1. Place all leather pieces on scrap paper or plastic. Use sheep's wool to apply two coats of buckskin dye. Allow to dry between coats.

2. Wrap the stain-coated wool around a 24" length of natural suede lace and pull to stain. (Photo 1)

3. Apply antiquing leather finish, following the manufacturer's instructions. Let dry.

4. Apply leather sheen to seal and finish. Let dry.

Photo 1 - Staining the leather lace with sheep's wool.

5. In a foam plate, mix a good amount of burnt umber acrylic paint with textile medium following manufacturer's instructions. Use a 1" paint brush to paint back side of leather with burnt umber acrylic paint. Let dry completely.

6. Apply leather balm to both sides of all leather surfaces, using a soft cloth. Buff to finish.

Construct:

1. Bend to curve the side edges of the tote into a vase shape, matching punched holes on the tabbed side extension with holes on the opposite side. Use short length of string or yarn to lace through a couple of holes at the top edge to hold in place. *Option:* Leather can be wet-formed to bend into shape.

Continued on page 114

Continued from page 113

2. Lace a 2-pronged needle with a 55" length of dark brown 1/8" grained leather lace. Beginning on inside of tote, insert needle through one bottom hole, going through both leather layers. Pull to outside of tote, leaving about 3" of lace on the inside. Continue to lace to top of tote through the punched holes. When you reach the top edge, return, criss-crossing your way to the bottom. **Do not** cut lacing.

3. Fold bottom flaps to create tote bottom. Layer shorter flaps between the longer flaps.

4. Thread the laced needle through layers to stitching holes along one edge of bottom and stitch in a criss-cross fashion as you did on the side. Bring the needle back through the layers to the side of the tote. Weave the lace through the previously stitched areas to secure and trim excess.

5. Stitch overlapped top ends of handles together in a criss-cross fashion, trapping the lace ends between the layers and stitches to secure.

6. Determine position of handle on tote. Mark, then punch 11/64" holes coordinating with handle holes found in leaves (about 3/4" from top edge).

7. Attach handles using short lengths of stained suede lace. Tie overhand knots to secure. ❏

Seed Pouch Tooling Pattern
(actual size)

Handle for Tool Tote
(Enlarge 200%)

Tooling Patterns
for Tool Tote
(actual size)

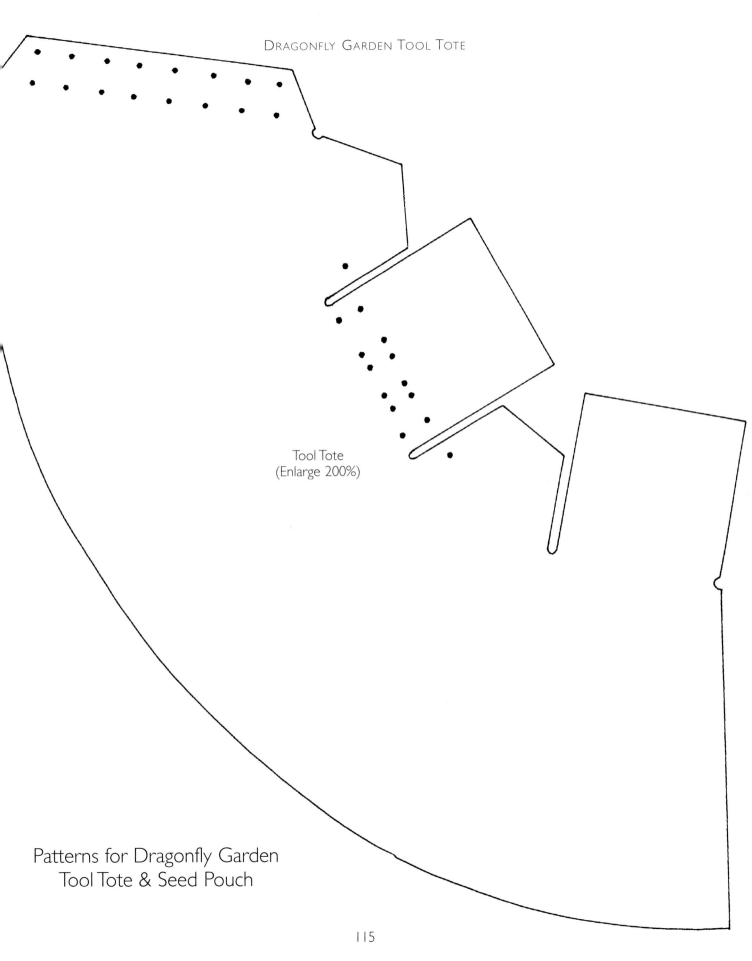

Tool Tote
(Enlarge 200%)

Patterns for Dragonfly Garden
Tool Tote & Seed Pouch

SUPPLIES

Leather:

Nature tanned leather
  1 piece, 24" x 12" (purse body)
  3 pieces, each 5" x 9-1/2"
  (gussets and flap)
  2 strips, each 2" x 29" (handles)
Dark brown grained leather lacing,
  1/8"
15" brown 2mm round leather lacing

Other Supplies:

Leather Dye - Tan
Super sheen leather finish
Poster board
Spray adhesive
60" cotton filler cord, 12/32"
3/8" wooden dowel, 6" length
Leathercrafting cement

Tools:

Leather shears
Rotary cutter
Cutting mat
Clear acrylic ruler
3-in-1 bone folder/creaser/slicker
2-prong lacing needle
Embroidery needle
Woodburning tool with teardrop-
  shaped shading tip and circle
  stamp tip
Metal baking sheet
Mallet
Round hole drive punch, 9/64"
Poly punching board
Sheep's wool scrap
Rubber gloves
Scrap paper or plastic
Binder clips
Handstitching awl with natural
  awl thread
Needlenose pliers
Saw
Drill and 1/16" drill bit
Fine grit sandpaper
Scissors

BRANDED LEATHER PURSE

The technique of using woodburning tools to "brand" decorative accents and design patterns into leather has been around for years. With the variety of interesting woodburning tips available, there couldn't be a better time to dabble in branding!

It's a good idea to practice with the woodburning tool on some scrap leather before working on your prepared leather surface. If you hold the branding iron too long against the leather, the leather will melt like butter, eventually creating a hole.

continued from page 116

INSTRUCTIONS

Cut:

1. Photocopy purse body pattern with punch guide, enlarging as directed. Photocopy gusset and flap pattern with punch guide. Attach patterns to poster board using spray adhesive. Cut out with scissors.

2. Binder clip patterns to leather pieces. Place on punch board and punch, using the 9/64" round hole drive punch and mallet. On flap piece **only**, turn punch template sideways, align template edge with un-punched flat edge of flap, and punch stitching holes, following template.

3. Round corners of handle strips.

4. Align side edge of purse body punch template along side edges of each strap. Punch an even row of stitching holes using the 9/64" drive punch.

5. Punch ends, using the template as a guide for spacing.

6. Mark, then drill two 1/16" holes in one end of wooden dowel - one hole 5/8" from end, the other 1-1/8" from same end.

Brand & Accent:

Use fine grit sandpaper as needed to remove charred buildup on end of wood-burning tips. Use needlenose pliers to change woodburning tips and place the hot tips on a metal baking sheet to cool. For best results, practice creating the design on a scrap of leather before working on your prepared leather pieces.

1. Place flap and handle pieces on a smooth surface. Plug in woodburning tool to heat.

2. Using the photo as a guide, brand the leather. The small dots are created with the tip of the wedge-shaped shader. (Photo 1)

3. Mark a line 1-7/8" from the drilled dowel end. Woodburn the design on the dowel. (Photo 2)

4. Run the flat edge of the shader across the surface to darken it.

5. Cut dowel at the 1-7/8" line.

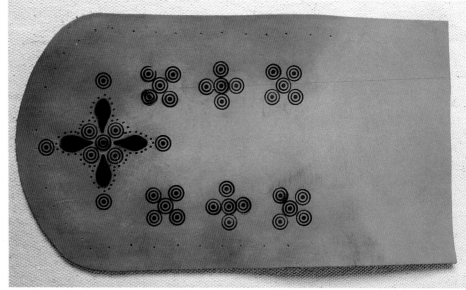

Photo 1 - The branded flap.

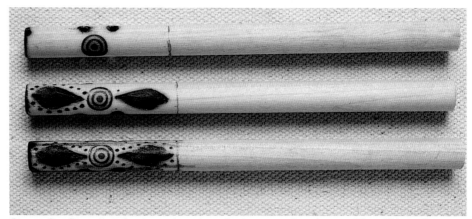

Photo 2 - Branding the wooden dowel to create the closure. The 6" length makes it easy to hold dowel as you work. When the woodburning is complete, the dowel can be cut to size.

6. Soften cut edges with shader tip. Brand a circle pattern at each end.

7. Lightly case leather with a dampened sponge. With a gloved hand, apply a small amount of tan dye to sheep's wool, dab off excess on scrap paper, and lightly apply, using a wiping motion. *Option:* Add more dye to highlight edges of flap. Let dry.

Construct:

1. With wrong sides together, binder clip side edges of purse to one gusset piece, aligning punched holes. Cut a length of dark brown grained lacing five-and-a-half times the bag length (here, 110"). Cut lace end in a wedge shape and insert in 2-prong needle.

2. Stitch gusset and purse together. Begin by bringing laced needle through back of first hole at top, leaving a 2" tail. Wrap around to bring needle through the first hole again, going through both leather layers. Pull taut. Stitch along side edges, trapping the tail between the stitches as you go. At opposite end, whipstitch once and stitch back to the starting point. Whipstitch once at end, insert needle through one leather layer and down between stitches approximately 2". Bring needle and remaining lace inside the purse. Trim excess.

3. Repeat to stitch second gusset on other side.

4. For flap, cut 60" of dark brown grained lacing and insert in 2-prong needle. Beginning on flat end, bring needle through a hole to top side of leather, leaving a 2" tail. Whipstitch once, then stitch all the way around the flap. When back at starting point, stitch back around the outer edge. Whipstitch once at end. Thread needle through back of lacing and trim excess.

5. To attach the handles, begin 3-1/2" from one handle end and bring needle through back side, leaving a 2" tail. Whipstitch once to hold in place, then stitch around handle end to the 3-1/2" mark opposite the starting point. Pull lacing taut.

6. Apply a thin bead of leathercrafting cement down the center of the handle's back side. Place cotton filler cord on cement. Continue to stitch handle, wrapping it around the filler cord as you stitch until you are 3-1/2" from the opposite end. Binder clip, if needed, as you work. Stitch around handle end, whipstitch at the 3-1/2" mark to secure end, and thread needle between stitches. Cut excess.

7. Repeat the process to stitch the second handle.

8. Use the stitching awl and natural awl thread to attach handles to purse, using the photo and lacing holes as guides to handstitch the leather layers together with a U-shaped line of stitching.

9. Use the stitching awl to stitch the flap to the back of the purse, beginning about 2-1/2" from top edge. Use lacing holes as stitching guides to create the rectangular-shaped handstitched reinforcement that holds the flap securely to the purse.

10. Insert 9" brown round lace through holes drilled in dowel, then through two lacing holes at bottom of flap. Knot at back.

11. Cut 6" brown round lace. Beginning on front of purse, insert ends through holes in front and knot at back to create a closure loop. Slip dowel through loop. ❏

LEFT: Progression of the branded motif.

Pattern for Branded
Leather Purse

Purse Body
Enlarge 250% for actual size

Gusset & Flap
(actual size)

RUSTIC RABBIT FUR BAG

Tattered, uneven edges of deer-tanned cowhide provide an attractive accent for this handbag. With its rabbit fur flap and artificial sinew stitching, it's a great casual bag for everyday use or as part of a costume for historical reenactments.

Due to variations in hides, no two handbags look exactly alike when finished. Adjust the stitching and overlap as needed to best suit the hide you're using. To make a purse that looks like mine, at least one 13" side edge should be from the tattered side edges of the deer-tanned hide. The edge does not need to be completely straight - in fact, it will look better if it's not.

SUPPLIES

Leather:

Deer-tanned cowhide

    1 piece, 22" x 13"

    2 pieces 1-1/4" x 15" (handle)

Natural rabbit skin

20" light rust cow suede lacing, 1/8"

Natural-toned artificial sinew, waxed, 30#

Other Supplies:

Leathercrafting cement

Poster board

Tools:

Leather shears

Rotary cutter with Victorian style cutting blade

Clear acrylic ruler

Cutting mat

Stitching awl

Round hold drive punch, 5/64"

Mallet

Poly punching board

Pencil

Scissors

Binder clips

INSTRUCTIONS

Prepare & Cut:

1. Trace around the 22" x 13" deer-tanned piece on poster board to create a pattern template. Set leather aside. Use scissors to cut out poster board template. (Fig. 1)

2. Bring 13" side edges of template together, with jagged edge overlapping opposite 13" edge near center. Use your palms to press the folded poster board to crease and mark the sides. Trace along jagged edge to mark overlap. (Fig. 2) Unfold.

3. Trim top edges of the template to create a U-shape on front for easy access into handbag and an upside-down U-shape on back that will be used to attach and reinforce the rabbit fur flap. (Fig. 3)

4. Use the stitching awl and punch board to mark, then punch a line of stitching holes about 1/2" apart at center of overlap. Punch through all layers of template.

5. With face side down, place template on leather, matching jagged side edges. Binder clip to attach. Use shears to cut leather, following template lines.

6. Punch stitching holes along side edges **only**. Remove poster board template.

Construct:

1. Thread needle with a length of artificial sinew one-and-a-half times the length of the center overlap. Knot end. Overlap the leather edges, matching the punched holes. Binder clip at top and bottom.

Continued on page 124

continued from page 122

Fig. 1 - The poster board template.

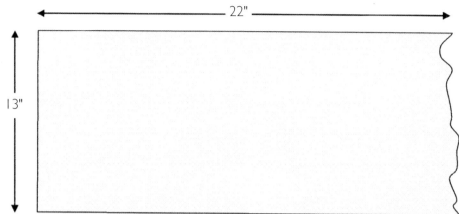

2. Beginning at inside-top edge, bring needle through back side of first hole through both layers. Whipstitch once to reinforce top edge, then use a running stitch to sew the overlapped edges to within 2" of bottom. **Do not** cut ends.

3. With threaded needle pulled to top of handbag, position the stitched overlap at center. Place handbag on cutting mat.

4. Place straight edge ruler 1/2" from handbag bottom. With rotary cutter with Victorian cutting blade, cut through both leather layers at the same time so that they will match up once stitched. (See Photo 1) TIP: For best results, binder clip bottom edge to hold cut edges together.

5. Finish stitching center overlap and whipstitch once at end to secure. Whipstitch on inside of handbag. Cut excess.

6. Cut a length of sinew 1-1/2 times the bottom width of the handbag and knot end. Use the stitching awl and punch

board to punch a row of stitches 3/8" from the bottom edge, 1/2" apart.

7. Beginning at one side edge on inside, bring needle through first hole and whipstitch, going through the first and second holes in both layers. Stitch bottom edge. Whipstitch at opposite end, bringing needle from between the layers, and whipstitch a couple more times. Trim ends.

Make Handle:

1. Use a pencil to mark a line 4" from one end of each leather handle piece.

2. With stitching awl and clear acrylic ruler, punch a line of stitching holes 1/4" from all outer edges of both handle pieces 1/2" apart.

3. Beginning at 4" marks on both pieces, punch another line of stitching along center of each piece, staggering the stitch holes between those punched at side edges.

4. Overlap opposite ends 1-1/2" to join the pieces. Thread needle with 90" of artificial sinew and knot end. Match stitching holes at overlap and, beginning at overlap, hand-stitch along side of strap to the 4" mark.

5. Cut light rust suede lace in half to make two 10" pieces. Loosely tie an overhand knot at each end. Center one piece on the back side of the handle, 2" from end. Fold end over the lace, bringing the back sides of the handle together, trapping the lace between the two layers. Match

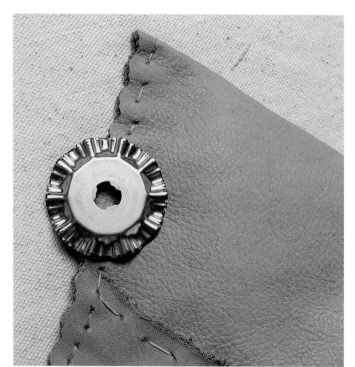

Photo 1 - The Victorian cutting blade.

Fig. 2 - Overlapping the template to form the purse shape. Bring the 13" edges together, overlapping at center with the jagged edge on top.

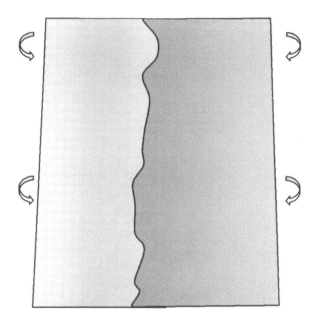

Fig. 3 - The trimmed template, with a U-shaped dip on the front and corresponding upside-down U-shape on the back to attach and reinforce the fur flap.

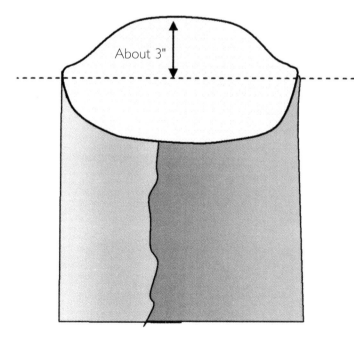

About 3"

stitching holes, then stitch to suede lace. Backstitch to starting point and continue to opposite handle end, repeating to trap the other suede lace piece 2" from opposite end. Stitch back to starting point. Whipstitch two to three times to secure thread ends, and cut excess. Repeat for opposite side edge of handle.

6. Thread needle with 110" of artificial sinew. Knot end. Beginning at 4" mark at one end of handle, bring needle through back side of first hole at handle center. Whipstitch once to secure, bringing needle to top side. Working one long edge at a time, fold outer edges of handle to center and whipstitch, bringing the threaded needle over the folded edge and back through the center row of punched stitching holes. When you reach the last hole (at the 4" mark on the opposite end), stitch handle's other side, creating a braided look. Once back at the starting point, whipstitch to secure ends. Cut excess.

7. Use the 5/64" drive punch, mallet, and punch board to punch two holes 1-1/2" apart at side edges of handbag, about 1" from top edge. Untie overhand knots at suede lace ends, and insert through punched holes on one side edge of handbag. Tie an overhand knot in one end of lace, adjust hang length, and knot remaining end. Trim excess lace. Repeat on opposite side.

Add Flap:

1. With the short flap of deer-tanned leather folded along the top, drape the rabbit fur over top edge to determine flap length and cut angle.

2. Mark the fur-lined hide on its back side, leaving about 1" extending beyond the top fold.

3. Cut rabbit fur by carefully sliding tip of shears along hide at base of fur. (This yields a more natural-looking cut that allows fur to cover the cut edge.

4. Apply leathercrafting cement to top of deer-tanned flap and adhere to back of rabbit fur hide.

5. Carefully handstitch fur to deer-tanned flap and back edge of handbag. (The white side edges of the fur hide can be turned under slightly and whipstitched to conceal them.) Whipstitch at ends to secure. Cut ends. ❏

METRIC CONVERSION CHART

Inches to Millimeters and Centimeters

Inches	MM	CM
1/8	3	.3
1/4	6	.6
3/8	10	1.0
1/2	13	1.3
5/8	16	1.6
3/4	19	1.9
7/8	22	2.2
1	25	2.5
1-1/4	32	3.2
1-1/2	38	3.8
1-3/4	44	4.4
2	51	5.1
3	76	7.6
4	102	10.2
5	127	12.7
6	152	15.2
7	178	17.8
8	203	20.3
9	229	22.9
10	254	25.4
11	279	27.9
12	305	30.5

Yards to Meters

Yards	Meters
1/8	.11
1/4	.23
3/8	.34
1/2	.46
5/8	.57
3/4	.69
7/8	.80
1	.91
2	1.83
3	2.74
4	3.66
5	4.57
6	5.49
7	6.40
8	7.32
9	8.23
10	9.14

INDEX